it's not about me

teen edition

Leader's Guide for Youth Workers

Len Woods

Based on *It's Not About Me, Teen Edition*

by Max Lucado

IT'S NOT ABOUT ME, Teen Edition
Leader's Guide for Youth Workers

Published by Integrity Publishers, a division of Integrity Media, Inc., 5250 Virginia Way, Suite 110, Brentwood, TN 37027.

HELPING PEOPLE WORLDWIDE EXPERIENCE the MANIFEST PRESENCE of GOD.

This leader's guide is based on and to be used in conjunction with *IT'S NOT ABOUT ME, Teen Edition,* © 2005 by Max Lucado. Published by Integrity Publishers.

Introductions and questions written by Len Woods.

Cover design by Brand Navigation, Portland, OR.

Interior design by Kirk Luttrell

Produced with the assistance of The Livingstone Corporation (www.LivingstoneCorp.com). Project staff include Dave Veerman, Kirk Luttrell, Mary Horner Collins, and Joel Bartlett.

ISBN 1-59145-312-7

Printed in the United States of America

05 06 07 08 09 DLT 9 8 7 6 5 4 3 2 1

contents

introduction

From advertising adages to political promises, pampered athletes to pompous performers, and music to movies, we are bombarded with self-centered messages. We hear and see that the world revolves around us and our needs. Young people are especially vulnerable to this message, as any parent of a teenager will readily attest. Teenagers often expect parents, teachers, coaches, youth leaders, friends, and everyone else to be sensitive to their desires and schedules.

Despite what the world tells us countless times daily, life is not about *us*. *We* are the not the point. The world doesn't revolve around *your* desires or *my* goals. And it was never meant to.

As Max Lucado states in *It's Not About Me, Teen Edition*, page 3:

> *When God looks at the center of the universe, he doesn't look at you. When heaven's stagehands direct the spotlight toward the star of the show, I need no sunglasses. No light falls on me.*
>
> *Lesser orbs, that's us. Appreciated. Valued. Loved dearly.*
>
> *But central? Essential? Critical? Nope. Sorry. The world does not revolve around us. Our comfort is not God's priority. If it is, something's gone wrong. If we are the primary event, how do we explain challenges like death, disease, or rumbling earthquakes? If God exists to please us, then shouldn't we always be pleased?*

You'd think we'd have figured out all this by now—a planet teeming with six billion self-absorbed, self-centered people, each operating by a philosophy that says, "It's all about *me*!" Why, that's nothing less than a recipe for total disaster and chaos!

Sure enough, look around you and what do you see? Cutthroat people. Wounded people. Bitter people. Restless people. Lonely people. Frustrated people. Disillusioned and unfulfilled people.

There's a much, much better way—if only we have ears to hear and hearts to follow. Life can begin to make sense—*if* we'll accept our proper place in the universe. We must begin to see everything—our pleasures, our problems, our gifts and talents—as being all for the One who created us. Only then do we gain what we've been missing and find what we've been seeking.

This is the only path to discovering the meaning-charged life our souls hunger for. And this is the transforming premise of *It's Not About Me*.

Now, with the publication of the teen edition of Max Lucado's best-selling book, we hope that young people will grasp early in life the revolutionary notion that they have been created by him and for him. And with this easy-to-use leader's guide, youth workers will now be able to introduce these life-altering concepts in a group setting.

The guide is intuitive and straightforward. It shows how to facilitate six meetings that explore the major concepts found in *It's Not About Me, Teen Edition*.

You will notice that each lesson plan contains most or all of the following components:

Primary Lesson Texts: list of the primary Bible passages to be studied in the session.

Lesson Focus/Key Concept: a simple statement of the main idea or takeaway truth of the session.

Lesson Goal: a clear objective for the group session.

Materials Needed: list of extra items needed to conduct a successful meeting.

Warmup/Openers: fun and creative exercises designed to get your group mixing, mingling and interacting—each one also intended to raise the central issue of the session.

Discussion: an often lighthearted, interactive entrée into the topic at hand.

Reading: a short excerpt from the *It's Not About Me, Teen Edition* book is recommended so that all students have a clear sense of the topic. It will be best if each student has his or her own copy of the book. You can teach the course without it, but you'll have to improvise in every lesson as the student book is used throughout. Group rates on the book are available.

Bible Study Discussion: a brief, focused time of reading, reflecting, and wrestling with the implications of God's Word.

Drama: short vignettes or improvisations intended for student performance, requiring little or no advance preparation.

Practical Application/Response: a final section or two intended to wrapup the meeting and call for some specific attitudinal and behavioral changes from the students.

Reproducible Worksheets: (highlighted in the Leader's section of each chapter) assorted ready-to-be-photocopied exercises for use in the meetings or for students to take home and complete. In this section, in every session, we have included INAM Weekly Devotions. This is an option for helping students continue the application of the session through the week.

Young Life® Adaptation: suggestions for using the session in a group where at least half of the students are not believers—an outreach-oriented group.

May God bless your efforts to help young people understand and live out the bottom-line reality of the universe: it's all about him! Amen!

Len Woods

the center of the universe

Primary Lesson Texts

Ephesians 1:20–22

Colossians 1:15–19 (This passage is not used in the *It's Not About Me, Teen Edition* book, but it strongly reinforces Christ as the center of all things.)

Matthew 6:9–13

Selected scriptures about the glory of God

Lesson Focus/Key Concept

The world does not revolve around me. My purpose in life is to reflect God's glory.

Lesson Goal

As a result of this session, students will begin to see that life is not about them but about God, and they will be challenged to begin to live God-centered lives. They will understand the difference between self-centeredness and self-worth.

Materials Needed

- ❑ Reproducible handouts, pages 12–20
- ❑ Pens/pencils
- ❑ An erasable marker board, markers, and an eraser
- ❑ 4 x 6 index cards
- ❑ TV (with cable hookup) or popular magazines (one per student)
- ❑ Blank sheets of 8 1/2 x 11 paper (one per student)

LEADER'S NOTES:

Warmup/Openers (10 minutes)

Choose one of the following openers.

❶ Brush with Greatness

For these activities, divide into smaller groups.

Give everyone a 4 x 6 index card and a pencil/pen. Instruct each student to quietly write down a true incident in which he or she had a "brush with greatness" (that is, an encounter with someone famous).

A sample "brush with greatness" might go like this: "I once met actor Tom Hanks in the Chicago airport and got his autograph on a ten-dollar bill."

After about three minutes, instruct everyone to finish up, to write their names on their cards, to fold the cards, and to give them to their group leaders.

The leader(s) will read the cards one at a time, and the group must try to guess the identity of the person who had that experience.

❷ IF

Use these "IF" questions to help your group begin to connect on a deeper level. Also, the exercise will help surface the various attitudes, values, and world-views of your students.

Be sure to allow for the time it will take to break into and out of groups.

Divide into smaller groups of 4–8 and have each group sit in a circle. Distribute copies of the "IF" sheet. The reproducible sheet is at the end of the session. Beginning with the person whose middle name has the fewest letters and moving counterclockwise (to the right), have first person answer the first question. Then next person should follow with the second question, and so on, until you signal that the time is up. If the group finishes before allotted time, have them all answer another question on list of their choice.

"IF"

- If the major TV networks gave you 60 seconds during prime time to promote any cause, how would you use that opportunity?
- If you could have any career (and be successful), what would you choose to do?
- If you suddenly inherited $10 million from some long-lost uncle, what would you do with the money?
- If you could have a private audience with the 100 most influential people in the world, what would you tell them?
- If you found out you had only one month left to live, how would you spend your final days?
- If you could ask God one question (and get an audible, understandable answer), what would you ask and why?
- If you were locked in a high-rise elevator for a weekend with two other people, whom would you prefer to be stuck with and why?
- If you could solve one giant world problem, which issue would you address and why?

- If you could have dinner with any four living people, which companions would you choose and why?
- If you had to give up some physical ability (for example, your eyesight or hearing), what would you give up and why?

Leader's Notes:

Discussion *(10 minutes)*

If you are meeting in a room that has TV/cable access, take about five minutes to do a little channel surfing. Stay on each channel for only a few seconds. Try to find a few commercials or, better yet, an infomercial. Encourage students to watch in a critical, detached way. Specifically, have them note what values, ideas, products, and so forth are being promoted on programs and commercials. What do the beliefs, culture, and lifestyles they are seeing tell them about the human race?

Be ready for this so all you have to do is turn on the television.

If you do not have TV/cable access, provide a stack of popular magazines—*Us*, *People*, *Seventeen*, *Vogue*, *GQ*, etc. Distribute the magazines, making sure that everyone has at least one. Tell them to thumb through the pages to get a feel for the values endorsed and championed by the publications.

If you use magazines, collect them afterward; otherwise they will become a major distraction.

When the time is up, have people report their observations.

- Ask:

"What did your research indicate?"

"What would you say this culture is into?"

"What are the values of these people? What do they care about? What do they seem to be giving their lives to?"

Jot these observations and comments on an erasable marker board (or have a volunteer do it).

Tell everyone to listen to this short, ancient, and very relevant Greek tale. Point out that you are talking about little *g* gods—not the one true God. Then have a volunteer read the following story:

> *Narcissus was unbelievably handsome. Every girl wanted him, but he wanted no one. He left broken hearts everywhere he went. One scorned maiden finally prayed to the gods, "May he who loves not others love himself."*
>
> *The goddess Nemesis heard this anguished and angry prayer and answered it. So one day, as Narcissus bent over a clear pool to get a drink, he saw his own reflection and fell head over heels in love—with himself!*
>
> *"Now I know," he cried, "what others have suffered from me, for I burn*

LEADER'S NOTES:

> *with love of my own self—and yet how can I reach that loveliness I see mirrored in the water? But I cannot leave it. Only death can set me free." And that is exactly what happened. Narcissus leaned perpetually over the pool, fixed in one continual gaze, pining away for his own image, until at last he died.*

Thank your reader. Then solicit some feedback from your students. Ask what they think about this myth. Is it an accurate picture of how most people live?

Say, "**We get our English word and modern concept of *narcissism* from this ancient story. A narcissist is one who is preoccupied, even obsessed, with self. Handsome or not, he is egocentric. Appearance aside, she thinks life is all about her.**

"**Truth be told, there is a stubborn streak of narcissism in all of us. Self-centeredness is the great legacy of humanity's rebellion against God (see Genesis 3). Hiding at the root of Self-Ish-Ness**" (write this word out on the erasable marker board) "**is—do you see it?—sin. And as long as we remain absorbed and consumed with our own small lives and petty desires, we will never find time or make time to acknowledge our great Creator or to be of service to our fellow creatures.**"

Ask where they see glaring examples of narcissism in our culture. (Bodybuilders admiring themselves in the wall-to-wall gym mirrors, people hung up on their appearance—increase in plastic surgery, shows like *Extreme Makeover*, *The Swan*, etc.)

Then ask if they know what an oxymoron is. Explain that an oxymoron is a phrase that combines contradictory or incongruous words—for example, *extra money*, *soft rock*. See if they can think of other common oxymorons.

Ask:

"**What about this oxymoron—'self-absorbed Christian?' Can there really be such a thing? Is such a lifestyle possible? Is it possible to be narcissistic and devoted to Christ? Why or why not?**"

"**Why are we—including many who call ourselves Christians—so wrapped up in ourselves?**"

Drama *(5 minutes)*

This will be most effective if rehearsed beforehand.

In advance, make copies of these "scripts"/scenarios—see the reproducible pages at the end of the session—to some of your more outgoing students and have them act them out for the group. (Pause between dramas for emphasis.)

Introduce this by saying, "Let's peek into the lives of some people struggling with real-life, everyday issues."

Scenario #1 (3 males)

Narrator: *Josh has been waiting all week for the big game. His favorite team just needs one victory to make the playoffs. Midway through the third quarter, with his team down by one and mounting a furious comeback, the game is preempted by a special news alert.*

Announcer: *We interrupt this program to bring you live coverage of a breaking news story. A four-alarm fire has engulfed an apartment building at the corner of Grafton and University streets downtown. Officials are reporting that as many as fifty-five people may be trapped in the upper floors of the structure.*

Josh: (yelling at the TV) *Aw, c'mon! We don't need live coverage—we can watch the highlights at 11:00. Aw, man! And we were just about to score! Gimme a break!*

Scenario #2 (1 male & 1 female)

Blaire: *So, now we're not going out tonight?!*

David: *Blaire, I really need to go by Craig's.*

Blaire: *Why tonight? Why can't you do it tomorrow? It's not like you guys are even close friends!*

David: *I know. That's true. We're not. But he is one of my teammates. Look, Blaire, the guy's dad died today. So . . . what? I'm gonna blow him off and go to a movie instead? How would that look? Everyone else on the team will be there.*

Blaire: *Yeah, well, what about our plans? I've been looking forward to this all week!*

David: *I know, me too. But what can I say? You act like I planned this.*

Blaire: *I'm not saying that.*

David: *Look, I'm sorry. Really. What do you want me to do?*

Blaire: *I want you to put me first for once. Just once.*

Afterward, thank your actors. Then ask:

"To which of these scenarios do you relate the most? Why?"

"Who is the most unselfish person you know? What do you attribute his/her unselfishness to?"

Bible Study Discussion (20 minutes)

Introduce this by saying, **"Listen up. What I'm about to read to you from *It's Not About Me, Teen Edition* is hard to hear. It's jarring. Shocking. But it will absolutely change your life if you believe it."** Read the following quote:

> *When God looks at the center of the universe, he doesn't look at you. When heaven's stagehands direct the spotlight toward the star of the show, I need no sunglasses. No light falls on me.*

Leader's Notes:

Leader's Notes:

> *Lesser orbs, that's us. Appreciated. Valued. Loved dearly.*
>
> *But central? Essential? Critical? Nope. Sorry. The world does not revolve around us. Our comfort is not God's priority. . . . God does not exist to make a big deal out of us. We exist to make a big deal out of him. It's not about you. It's not about me. It's all about him.*

Then say: "**To people living in a loud, fast, flashy world, God speaks quietly through the pages of the Bible about the way things really are. Think of these Bible passages as little windows of ultimate Truth. Think of them as God pulling back the curtains and giving us a glimpse of what really matters.**"

God Is Central!

Print out these verses and hand them to students beforehand, so they can be ready to read aloud. Have students read these passages aloud, one at a time:

God raised [Christ] from death and set him on a throne in deep heaven, in charge of running the universe, everything from galaxies to governments, no name and no power exempt from his rule. And not just for the time being but forever. He is in charge of it all, has the final word on everything. At the center of all this, Christ rules the church (Ephesians 1:20–22 MSG).

This next passage is not found in the *It's Not About Me, Teen Edition*, but it is applicable to the discussion.

He is the image of the invisible God, the firstborn over all creation. For by him all things were created: things in heaven and on earth, visible and invisible, whether thrones or powers or rulers or authorities; all things were created by him and for him. He is before all things, and in him all things hold together. And he is the head of the body, the church; he is the beginning and the firstborn from among the dead, so that in everything he might have the supremacy. (Colossians 1:15–18 NIV)

Divide into groups of four and distribute copies of the Bible Study Discussion Sheet, which has those passages and the following discussion questions:

- What's your gut reaction to these passages? Have you ever heard anything like this before?
- According to these Bible passages, who or what is the focal point of the universe? Does this seem true in everyday life? In your life?
- In what ways do these verses contradict what the world says about who's in charge?
- Why don't people see this truth and adjust? Why do people who are Christians so often forget this truth?

This discussion should take about 5 minutes.

After a few minutes, pull the group back together. Then say, "**Now, let's look at some passages that teach that God is about promoting God!**"

Read aloud the following verses:

[God himself speaking] By those who come near Me I must be regarded as holy; and before all the people I must be glorified. (Leviticus 10:3 NKJV)

[King David speaking] Declare his glory among the nations, his marvelous deeds among all peoples. (1 Chronicles 16:24 NIV)

Then say, "**We find these words in the *It's Not About Me, Teen Edition* book,**" and read aloud the following:

> *When you think "God's glory," think "priority." For God's glory is God's priority.*
>
> *God's team meetings, if he had them, would revolve around one question: "How can we reveal my glory today?" God's to-do list consists of one item: "Reveal my glory." Heaven's framed and mounted purpose statement hangs in the angels' break room just above the angel food cake. It reads: "Declare God's glory."*

Then say, "**A skeptic might ask: 'Why is God so obsessed with getting glory? Is he insecure? Is he arrogant? When people demand glory and honor, we call them ego-maniacs. Why shouldn't we think the same of God?' How do you respond?**"

After your students bat this question around for a few minutes, say: "**In his book *Desiring God*, pastor John Piper says:** "People stumble over the teaching that God exalts his own glory and seeks to be praised by his people [because] the Bible teaches us not to be like that. . . . How can God be . . . so utterly for himself?

The answer I propose is this: Because God is unique as an all-glorious, totally self-sufficient Being, he must be for himself if he is to be for us. The rules of humility that belong to a creature cannot apply in the same way to its Creator. If God should turn away from himself as the Source of infinite joy, he would cease to be God. He would deny the infinite worth of his own glory. He would imply that there is something more valuable outside himself. He would commit idolatry.

This would be no gain for us. For where can we go when our God has become unrighteous?"

Ask:
"What strikes you about that explanation?"

"Does it make sense to you? Why or why not?"

Ask your students to track with and interact with the following argument:

"If God *is* the source of absolute truth and ultimate righteousness, if he

LEADER'S NOTES:

LEADER'S NOTES:

really *is* the most glorious being in all the universe, if there is no one and nothing else like him, if he *is* the One who intrinsically deserves ultimate honor and praise, then wouldn't it be wrong for him *not* to promote that fact? If he built us to order our lives around him and find true fulfillment in him, wouldn't it be wrong for him to *not* say and seek that? Wouldn't it be illogical and bizarre for our awesome Creator to be unbothered when we ignore his infinite worth and, instead, worship unworthy things?"

Ask: **"Do you agree or disagree? Why?"**

Practical Application *(7 minutes)*

Spend a few minutes making a case for why God must declare his greatness and why he must demand our worship.

Say: **"The next time we gather, we're going to look more closely at God's glorious nature and how and why we worship. But for now, let me close this session by reading to you from the *It's Not About Me, Teen Edition* (p. 7)."** Have students follow along in their books.

For most of us, such a shift [from a me-centered lifestyle to a God-centered one] doesn't come easily. We've been demanding our way and stamping our feet since infancy. Aren't we all born with a default drive set on selfishness? "I want a family that lets me have my way and friends who always agree with me. It's all about me."

Promote me. Take care of me. Focus on me. It's all about me!

Aren't we urged to look out for number one? Find our place in the sun? Make a name for ourselves? We thought celebrating ourselves would make us happy . . .

But what chaos this philosophy creates. If you think it's all about you, and I think it's all about me, we have no hope for getting along.

What would happen if we took our places and played our parts in this universe? If we played the parts God gave us to play? If that was our highest priority?

Would we see a change in our families? We'd certainly hear a change. Less "Here is what I want!" More "What do you suppose God wants?"

What if you took that approach? Goals of being popular and part of the in-crowd—you'd shelve them. God-reflecting would dominate.

And your body? Worldly thinking says, "It's mine; I'm going to enjoy it." God-centered thinking acknowledges, "It's God's; I have to respect it."

You'd see suffering differently. "My pain proves God's absence" would be replaced with "My pain expands God's purpose."

Talk about a shift. Life makes sense when we accept our place. The gift of pleasures, the purpose of problems—all for him. The God-centered life works. And it rescues us from a life that doesn't.

But how do we make the shift? How can we be bumped off self-center? We move from me-focus to God-focus by pondering him. Witnessing him. Following the counsel of the apostle Paul: "Beholding as in a glass the glory of the Lord, [we] are changed into the same image from glory to glory, even as by the Spirit of the Lord." (2 Corinthians 3:18 KJV)

Beholding him changes us. Couldn't we use a change? Let's give it a go. Who knows? We might just discover our place in the universe.

Afterward, have everyone think or hand out a notecard to jot down the changes of putting God first might require in their lives. Explain that you and the other staff will be happy to talk one-on-one about how to make that happen.

Leader's Notes:

Make sure that everyone is quiet and taking this seriously. You may want to distribute index cards so they can jot down the possible changes.

Response *(8 minutes)*

Prayer

Hand out copies of this version of the Lord's Prayer from the reproducible pages. Then pray the prayer together, aloud.

Our Father in heaven,
*may **your** name be honored.*
*May **your** Kingdom come soon.*
*May **your** will be done here on earth,*
just as it is in heaven.
Give us our food for today,
and forgive us our sins,
just as we have forgiven those who have sinned against us.
And don't let us yield to temptation,
but deliver us from the evil one.

(Jesus speaking in Matthew 6:9–13 NLT; emphasis added)

Leader's Notes:

Wrap Up

Play the song "Show Me Your Glory" (Third Day, *Come Together*, Essential Records, 2001) while everyone listens quietly.

If you have additional time in your session, select one of the activities from the INAM Experiment (p. 17) to do together as a group. Otherwise, hand out a copy of INAM Experiment, assign an experiment, and ask students to complete one of the Experiments before your next meeting.

Distribute the "It's Not About Me Group Covenant" sheets. Encourage students to sign them and turn them in.

Explain and distribute the INAM Weekly Devotions. Ask students to bring with them completed devotionals next session as a means of accountability. (The devotional sheets are not included in the group session's activities.)

Close in prayer.

REPRODUCIBLE WORKSHEETS for Session 1

"IF"

- If the major TV networks gave you 60 seconds during prime time to promote any cause, how would you use that opportunity?
- If you could have any career (and be successful), what would you choose to do?
- If you suddenly inherited $10 million from some long-lost uncle, what would you do with the money?
- If you could have a private audience with the 100 most influential people in the world, what would you tell them?
- If you found out you had only one month left to live, how would you spend your final days?
- If you could ask God one question (and get an audible, understandable answer), what would you ask and why?
- If you were locked in a high-rise elevator for a weekend with two other people, whom would you prefer to be stuck with and why?
- If you could solve one giant world problem, which issue would you address and why?
- If you could have dinner with any four living people, which companions would you choose and why?
- If you had to give up some physical ability (for example, your eyesight or hearing), what would you give up and why?

Drama Scripts

Scenario #1 (3 males)

Narrator: *Josh has been waiting all week for the big game. His favorite team just needs one victory to make it to the playoffs. Midway through the third quarter, with his team down by one and mounting a furious comeback, the game is preempted by a special news alert.*

Announcer: *We interrupt this program to bring you this live coverage of a breaking news story. A four-alarm fire has engulfed an apartment building at the corner of Grafton and University streets downtown. Officials are reporting that as many as fifty-five people may be trapped in the upper floors of the structure.*

Josh (yelling at the TV): *Aw, c'mon! We don't need live coverage—we can watch the highlights at 11:00. Aw, man! And we were just about to score! Gimme a break!*

Scenario #2 (1 male & 1 female)

Blaire: *So, now we're not going out tonight?*

David: *Blaire, I really need to go by Craig's.*

Blaire: *Why tonight? Why can't you do it tomorrow? It's not like you guys are even close friends!*

David: *I know. That's true. We're not. But he is one of my teammates. Look, Blaire, the guy's dad died today. So . . . what? I'm gonna blow him off and go to a movie instead? How would that look? Everyone else on the team will be there but me.*

Blaire: *Yeah, well, what about our plans? I've been looking forward to this all week!*

David: *I know, me too. But what can I say? You act like I planned this all out.*

Blaire: *I'm not saying that.*

David: *Look, I'm sorry. Really. What do you want me to do?*

Blaire: *I want you to put me first for once. Just once.*

Bible Study Discussion Sheet

God raised [Christ] from death and set him on a throne in deep heaven, in charge of running the universe, everything from galaxies to governments, no name and no power exempt from his rule. And not just for the time being but forever. He is in charge of it all, has the final word on everything. At the center of all this, Christ rules the church (Ephesians 1:20–22 MSG).

He is the image of the invisible God, the firstborn over all creation. For by him all things were created: things in heaven and on earth, visible and invisible, whether thrones or powers or rulers or authorities; all things were created by him and for him. He is before all things, and in him all things hold together. And he is the head of the body, the church; he is the beginning and the firstborn from among the dead, so that in everything he might have the supremacy (Colossians 1:15–18 NIV).

- What's your gut reaction to these passages? Have you ever heard anything like this before?

- According to these Bible passages, who or what is the focal point of the universe? Does this seem true in everyday life? In your life?

- In what ways do these verses contradict what the world says about who's in charge?

- Why don't people see this truth and adjust? Why do people who are Christians so often forget this truth?

Prayer

Our Father in heaven,

may ***your*** *name be honored.*

May ***your*** *Kingdom come soon.*

May ***your*** *will be done here on earth,*

just as it is in heaven.

Give us our food for today,

and forgive us our sins,

just as we have forgiven those who have sinned against us.

And don't let us yield to temptation,

but deliver us from the evil one.

(Matthew 6:9–13 NLT; emphasis added)

Prayer

Our Father in heaven,

may ***your*** *name be honored.*

May ***your*** *Kingdom come soon.*

May ***your*** *will be done here on earth,*

just as it is in heaven.

Give us our food for today,

and forgive us our sins,

just as we have forgiven those who have sinned against us.

And don't let us yield to temptation,

but deliver us from the evil one.

(Matthew 6:9–13 NLT; emphasis added)

It's Not About Me Group Covenant

Purpose

Our purpose is to spend six sessions/weeks reading, discussing, pondering, and applying the concepts presented in the book *It's Not About Me, Teen Edition.* We want to explore what it means to live a God-centered life.

Goals

By the end of this six-part series:

- Members will better understand what it means to live for God's glory.
- Members will have a different (that is, a more biblically accurate) view of the greatness of God.
- Members will see the importance of spreading God's message.
- Members will understand how to glorify God in their bodies.
- Members will grasp how God deserves all our devotion in good times and bad.
- Members will be faced with the life-altering decision of whether to live wholeheartedly for God.

Commitments

By participating in this group, I am committing to:

- Preparing in advance (reading the book chapter and doing all take-home assignments).
- Showing up on time for our meetings and participating honestly in the discussions.
- Listening humbly to others and trying to encourage them to pursue God more deeply.
- Being available to those in the group for support, discussion, etc. outside of our meeting times.
- Allowing my group members to hold me accountable for any goals I set or commitments I make.

Signature ______________________________

Date __________________

THE INAM EXPERIMENT

Use the following list of take-home miniprojects this next week to help you get a better handle on the God-centered mind-set and lifestyle.

1. Find a beautiful place near your home (for example, a lakefront, a park, an overlook) and go there, maybe at sunrise or sunset. Spend time marveling at the glory and majesty of God revealed in his creation.

2. Read Psalms 95–100 or 145–150 in a different translation or contemporary paraphrase of the Bible.

3. Look for glimpses of God's glory in the people with whom you interact all day. Instead of focusing on their quirks and failures, notice instead the image of God in them.

4. Get up early and spend some time just lingering in God's presence. C. S. Lewis wrote in *Mere Christianity*: "The real problem of the Christian life comes . . . the very moment you wake up each morning. All your wishes and hopes for the day rush at you like wild animals. And the first job each morning consists simply in shoving them all back; in listening to that other voice, taking that other point of view, letting that other larger, stronger, quieter life come flowing in." Push back those distractions. Be still. Listen. Ask God to show you his glory.

5. Get out your daily schedule. Looking at your own calendar and your scheduled activities, ask and answer these same questions:

   - *How might I give God glory today in and through all these planned events, appointments, and meetings?*
   - *What if these plans fall apart or go awry? How can I continue to bring honor to God?*
   - *How can I put the righteous reputation of God on display in my unique circumstances?*

6. Somewhere you probably have a scrapbook or box full of old photographs. Take a few minutes to look through the box. Stroll down "memory lane." Do you find yourself skipping hurriedly over snapshots that do not include you? Why? What does this suggest?

7. During this next week, look for evidence of self-centeredness in your actions and attitudes. Watch out for those situations where you typically expect to be served instead of to serve, where you are prone to take rather than to give, and where you push (and even manipulate) others to meet your agenda.

INAM WEEKLY DEVOTIONS

The following scene takes place right at the beginning of Jesus's public ministry.

A former carpenter from Nazareth, Israel, Jesus has just begun to preach and do jaw-dropping miracles. People have never seen or heard anyone like him. Folks are intrigued and amazed. "Could this be the Christ (the long-awaited Messiah) and Savior sent by God?"

Peter, Andrew, James, and John have had some prior experience with Jesus (see John 1:35–51), hanging out with him, listening to him, and observing his actions.

Got all that? Okay. Now, read this passage thoughtfully each day, and answer the questions that follow:

> *One day as Jesus was walking along the shore beside the Sea of Galilee, he saw two brothers—Simon, also called Peter, and Andrew—fishing with a net, for they were commercial fishermen. Jesus called out to them, "Come, be my disciples, and I will show you how to fish for people!" And they left their nets at once and went with him.*
>
> *A little farther up the shore he saw two other brothers, James and John, sitting in a boat with their father, Zebedee, mending their nets. And he called them to come, too. They immediately followed him, leaving the boat and their father behind (Matthew 4:18–22 NLT).*

Day 1

- Who is doing the inviting here, and to what are the men being invited?

____

____

____

____

- What does the invitation require of these men? If accepted, how will this opportunity change their lives?

____

____

____

____

____

____

____

Day 2

- Why doesn't Jesus give more details about what following him will involve?

- What word(s) do you think describe how these fishermen felt as they responded (circle all that apply and explain your answer):

scared excited anxious relieved confused other:

Day 3

- Would it have been possible for these men to follow Jesus while staying where they were or without altering their lives?

- Can we follow Jesus but continue to insist on following the course we have chosen for our own lives? Why or why not?

Day 4

When, if ever, did you first “meet” Jesus? What were the circumstances?

Day 5

What is the difference in saying, “Christ, I will follow your lead and live out your agenda” and saying, “Christ, I want you to help me accomplish my dreams”?

Young Life® Adaptation for Session 1

Recommended for Wyldlife® Small Groups

This adaptation assumes a meeting designed primarily for enhancing relationships with students and for pre-evangelism.

Use the opener "Brush with Greatness." This should be fun and not threatening to anyone.

Next, do the *Discussion* as presented, but move right into the *Drama* immediately after you discuss the questions that follow the TV viewing (or magazine analysis). In other words, skip over the story of Narcissus and the discussion of oxymorons.

For the *Bible Study Discussion* section, go ahead and have students read aloud the Bible passages, but don't break into groups. Discuss the passages as a large group, and then finish the section as it is presented.

Use the *Practical Application* section as written. With *Response,* however, have four to six kids whom you know are Christians come up and read aloud the Lord's Prayer from Matthew 6, rather than having the group pray it together. This will avoid confusing or offending kids from a variety of religious backgrounds.

Because this is the first session, explain the "It's Not About Me Group Covenant." If you feel your group is up to it, distribute copies. Also, you may want to point out the "INAM Experiment" sheet and the INAM Weekly Devotions as options for going deeper. You might choose to forego distribution of those sheets but make them available.

Recommended for Young Life Campaigners

This adaptation assumes a meeting designed for Young Life Senior High Campaigner groups. The attendees will be primarily new believers with little or no church background.

Do the *Discussion* with TV and/or magazines (10–13 minutes).

Next, use the *Bible Study Discussion* section as it is (15–20 minutes).

Move into the *Practical Application* (7–10 minutes).

Close by distributing the "It's Not About Me Group Covenant" sheets. Encourage students to sign them and turn them in. Mention the INAM Weekly Devotions for those interested. Then, if you have time, play the song "Show Me Your Glory" (Third Day) while everyone listens quietly (3–7 minutes).

glimpses of God

Primary Lesson Texts
Exodus 15:11
Exodus 33
Psalm 19:1
Romans 11:36

Lesson Focus/Key Concept
God is glorious! He deserves all our attention, affection, and adoration. When our deepest desire in life is not a favor from God, but God himself, we cross a threshold. Less self-focus; more God-focus. Less about me; more about him.

Lesson Goal
As a result of this lesson, students will catch a glimpse of God's glory, and they will resolve to worship him fully with their lives.

Materials Needed
- ❑ Reproducible handouts, pages 34–40
- ❑ Pens/pencils
- ❑ Tongue twisters on slips of paper
- ❑ Bibles
- ❑ Prize

LEADER'S NOTES:

Warmup/Openers (10 minutes)

People Pandemonium (good for larger groups)

This icebreaker combines crazy activity with opportunities for getting acquainted. It also subtly reminds us of how easy it is to spend our lives caught up in trivial activities that don't matter. It will be most effective in larger groups.

Give each person a copy of the People Pandemonium handout (see the reproducible sheets section at the end of the session).

PEOPLE PANDEMONIUM

Instructions: As quickly and accurately as possible, accomplish each of the following items and secure required signature. You do not have to complete them in order.

- Find someone who has (or had) braces and get him or her to say "CHEESE!" while you pretend to take his or her picture. That person signs here:
- Get with two other people and do your best impersonation of supermodels walking down a runway during a fashion show (must walk all the way across the room). One of your threesome signs here:
- Find a partner and pretend to ride a bicycle built for two around the room—backward. Your cycling companion signs here:
- Try to breakdance or moonwalk and get a witness to sign here:
- Get the initials of someone who can imitate someone famous (Note: They must do their impersonation for you):
- Find someone who is smiling or laughing, introduce yourself, and get that person to sign here:
- Grab a partner, exchange names, then drop down and do fifteen push-ups or crunches. Stand back up and high-five each other. Sign each other's sheet here:
- Stand on a chair and give an impassioned 15-second speech on "How People Spend Their Precious Lives Doing Trivial Things." When you're finished, sign here:

Wrap this up by reminding teens that these were fun but not important activities. We can fill our days with unimportant, trivial activities and fail to focus on the most important things in life.

You may want to see who can say each phrase correctly the quickest.

Discussion (10 minutes)

Restore a sense of order and award a prize to the winner. Then say, **"Okay, let's test our verbal abilities with a little tongue-twister competition."**

Have four or five volunteers come forward. Pull the following tongue twisters (printed out on slips of paper) out of a hat. Ham it up and make a big fuss about who is the most articulate and adept enunciator. Add an extra competitive element by pitting the guys against the girls.

- Friendly Frank flips fine flapjacks.
- Fat frogs flying past fast.
- We surely shall see the sun shine soon.
- Six shimmering sharks sharply striking shins.
- Chop shops stock chops.
- Plague-bearing prairie dogs.
- Good blood, bad blood.
- Cedar shingles should be shaved and saved.
- Listen to the local yokel yodel.
- Are our oars oak?
- Please pay promptly.
- What time does the wrist watch strap shop shut?
- Girl gargoyle, guy gargoyle.
- Two toads, totally tired.
- Freshly fried flying fish.
- Strange strategic statistics.
- Six slippery snails slid slowly seaward.
- Three twigs twined tightly.
- Shredded Swiss cheese.
- The soldiers shouldered shooters on their shoulders.
- Irish wrist watch.
- Fred fed Ted bread, and Ted fed Fred bread.
- Cows graze in groves on grass, which grows in grooves in groves.

Say: **"That was fun, but here's a tongue twister I want us to think about as we move into our lesson:**

God's great glory grows grander."

Ask them to say this several times, speeding up each time.

Then say: **"And guess what. That last one is harder to do than it is to say. It's not just a tongue twister; it's a life twister. How do we bring God ever-increasing glory? How do we live in such a way that people ooh and aah over our God? That's our theme in this session."**

LEADER'S NOTES:

Leader's Notes:

Reading *(7 minutes)*

Say: **"Last time we wrestled with the concept that life is *not* about us. It's all about God. He is the center of the universe—not us. He doesn't exist for us; we exist for him. Today we want to carry those ideas further." We'll discuss, "What is God really like, and how should we respond to him? What does it mean to say that God is *glorious*? What does it mean to *worship*?"**

To refresh everyone's memories (or to bring people up to speed who haven't read) and to set the context for this session, read the following excerpt from chapter 2 (p. 14) of *It's Not About Me, Teen Edition*. Students may want to follow along in their books.

> *An anxious Moses needs help. This one-time shepherd has just conducted the largest mass exodus in history, leading a million people out of Egypt, out of slavery—and straight into a wilderness. To say the least, things haven't gone smoothly. So Moses pleads with God for help. "Look, you tell me, 'Lead this people,' but you don't let me know whom you're going to send with me. . . . Are you traveling with us or not?" (Exodus 33:12, 16 MSG).*
>
> *His Maker offers assurance. "I myself will go with you. . . . I will do what you ask, because I know you very well, and I am pleased with you" (vv. 14, 17 NCV).*
>
> *You'd think that would have been enough for Moses, but he lingers. Thinking, perhaps, of that last sentence: "I will do what you ask . . ." Perhaps God will allow one more request. So Moses swallows, sighs, and requests . . .*
>
> *What do you think he will ask for? He has God's attention. God seems willing to hear his prayer.*
>
> *So many requests he could make. There are a million stiff-necked, unappreciative, cow-worshiping ex-slaves in his rearview mirror who grumble with every step (Exodus 12:37). Had Moses prayed, "Could you turn these people into sheep?" who would have blamed him?*
>
> *And what about Israel's enemies? Battlefields in Canaan lie ahead. Combat with Hittites, Jebusites . . . Termites, and Cellulites. They infest the land. Can Moses mold an army out of pyramid-building Hebrews? Had Moses prayed, "Could you just beam us to Canaan?" who would have blamed him?*
>
> *Moses knew what God could do. The entire Ancient East knew. They were still talking about Aaron's staff becoming a snake and the Nile becoming blood. The plagues had brought air so thick with gnats you breathed them. Ground so layered with locusts you crunched them. Noonday blackness. Hail-pounded crops. Flesh covered with boils. Funerals for the firstborn.*
>
> *God had even turned the Red Sea into a red carpet. Yes, Moses knew what God could do.*

So with grumbling Israelites behind him and dangerous Canaanites in front of him, what is Moses' one request to God? "Show me your glory" (Exodus 33:18 NCV).

We cross a line when we make such a request. When our deepest desire is not the things of God, or a favor from God, but God himself, we cross a threshold. Less self-focus, more God-focus. Less about me, more about him.

"Show me your radiance," Moses is praying. "Flex your biceps. Let me see the S on your chest. Your preeminence.

Your heart-stopping, ground-shaking extraspectacularness. Forget good looks and athletic ability. Bypass the great GPA. I can live without them, but I can't live without you. I want more God, please. I'd like to see more of your glory."

Afterward ask: **"Why do you think Moses wanted to see God's greatness?"**

Bible Study Discussion *(10 minutes)*

Beforehand, ask students to stand and read the following passages aloud. They can be found on a reproducible sheet at the end of the session.

God Is Glorious!

The heavens declare the glory of God. (Psalm 19:1 NIV)

Who among the gods is like you, O LORD? Who is like you—majestic in holiness, awesome in glory, working wonders? (Exodus 15:11 NIV)

Declare his glory among the nations, his marvelous deeds among all peoples. (1 Chronicles 16:24 NIV)

God made all things, and everything continues through him and for him. To him be the glory forever. (Romans 11:36 NCV)

You can lead the discussion with the whole group, or you may want to break into small groups and have students discuss among themselves. If you choose the latter, distribute copies of the reproducible sheet at the end of the lesson.

Have the students briefly discuss these passages by working through the following questions:

- Why do you think the Bible puts such an emphasis on the glory of God?
- What exactly is God's glory? How would you describe it? What kind of effect does the word "glory" produce in your mind?
- What does it mean to "glorify" God? How would you explain these concepts to a child? To an unbelieving friend?

LEADER'S NOTES:

When you ask students to be your readers, have them practice reading with you so you can help them with inflection, etc.

Remember, breaking into and out of small groups takes time.

Leader's Notes:

Say, **"In *It's Not About Me, Teen Edition*** [p. 25], **Max Lucado notes that the Hebrew term for *glory* comes from a root word meaning 'heavy, weighty, or important.' In other words, God's glory celebrates his significance, his uniqueness, his one-of-a-kindness.**

"The *It's Not About Me, Teen Edition* [p. 4] **uses the moon and sun to speak about our place in the universe and to illustrate what it means to glorify God."** (It would be good to draw a picture of the sun and moon or hold up pictures to give students a visual focus.) **Max writes:**

> *What does the moon do? She generates no light. Contrary to the lyrics of the song, this harvest moon cannot shine on. Apart from the sun, the moon is nothing more than a pitch-black, pockmarked rock. But properly positioned, the moon beams. Let her do what she was made to do, and a clod of dirt becomes a source of inspiration and romance. The moon reflects the greater light.*
>
> *And she's happy to do so! You never hear the moon complaining. She makes no waves about making waves. Let the cow jump over her or astronauts step on her; she never objects. Even though sunning is accepted while mooning is the butt of bad jokes, you won't hear ol' Cheeseface grumble. The moon is at peace in her place. And because she is, soft light touches a dark earth.*

Ask:

"In what ways are we created like the moon? How should we function like the moon?"

"What does it mean for a person to be a 'reflector'? Give some specific examples."

Dramas *(5 minutes)*

Choose students who have experience in acting or speech.

Beforehand, recruit three appropriate students to help with these dramas. Have them come forward and improvise the following scenarios. (Note: Each of these scenarios touches on the issues of glory and/or praise.)

❶ *The Big Game*

The Situation: The students are rabid fans cheering on their high school basketball team to mount a fourth-quarter comeback from sixteen points behind. They are unashamedly "praising" the performance of the team.

The Stipulation: The actors must speak with an agreed-upon accent.

❷ *The Hospital Waiting Room*

The Situation: The students have just gotten the news that one of their friends has miraculously survived a near-fatal car wreck. They are thankful, grateful, in awe.

The Stipulation: The actors can only speak in questions; that is, each line they improvise must be in the form of a question.

❸ *The Coffee Shop*

The Situation: The students are hanging out, drinking lattes and cowriting a message about God's glory.

The Stipulation: Each actor can speak only two words in a row, then the next actor, then the next, and so forth.

Afterward, ask: **"What's the point of this exercise? What are these little improv dramas all about?"**

Let students give some suggestions. Then say: **"Each of these skits deals with some aspect of worship or God's glory. In the first one, the students were investing themselves—their energy and attention and, so to speak, their affection and devotion in cheering on their beloved team. They were *praising* the players' performance. They were *enjoying* their team. Is this what we do when we sing or give praises to God?**

"In the second drama, the students were appropriately looking to God as the one to whom all gratitude and honor are due.

"In the third, the students were attempting to describe or advertise God's glory. They were collaborating to make known the greatness of God, which is—in a real sense—what we are supposed to be about."

Practical Application (12 minutes)

Break up into smaller groups (3–5 people) and work through this sheet. (If you run out of time, encourage everyone to make an appointment to get together with one or two members of the group sometime within the week to finish this discussion.)

Ten Transforming Truths about Worship

❶ **In its purest sense, worship is simply assigning worth or value to someone or something.** Why do we say this? Because the word *worship* actually derives from the Old English term *worthship* (the state of having worth or value).

- *What thoughts, words, and images come to mind when you think of the word* worship?
- *How would you define worship to an unchurched person who asked, "Why do you Christians sing about God every Sunday morning? What's up with that?"*

❷ **Worship involves the glad and lavish giving of our devotion.** That is, when we view

Leader's Notes:

At each point, make this practical. That is, you might ask, "What should this mean to us, how we worship?"

LEADER'S NOTES:

someone or something as valuable, we eagerly devote our time, our allegiance, our affection, our emotional energy, our material resources, our praise to that person or thing.

- *Can you think of other specific ways people express their devotion?*
- *Why do we say that worship is "glad"? (Hint: Think of avid football fans or young couples in love.) Why do we say that worship is "lavish"?*

❸ **Everyone in the world is a worshiper.** That is, we all have relationships or things in our lives we consider valuable and usually one person or thing we view as having supreme worth. It is not a question of "*Will* I worship?" but rather "*Who* or *what* will I worship?"

- *In what ways is this a new concept for you?*
- *Have you ever stopped to consider this idea before—that everyone on this planet worships someone or something?*

❹ **Not everyone in the world worships *God*.** (This statement shouldn't need any explanation!)

- *What, in your opinion, are the most common objects of worship among Americans?*
- *Now forget about relationships and objects. Think in terms of ideals (for example, comfort, pleasure, etc.). What are some other similar ideals to which many are devoted?*

❺ **What a person (truly) worships can be easily discovered.** That is, it's not hard to look at a person's life and tell what he or she values above all else. Look at his calendar or schedule book, listen to her conversation, and observe how he spends his money and emotions, and you will have a good indication of what the person considers to have the highest worth.

- *Why is it common for people to worship "self"?*
- *In what ways might people value "Christianity" more than "Christ"?*

❻ **The Bible speaks of God, our Creator and Redeemer, as the One who alone deserves our worship.** (Read Revelation 4:8–11; 7:9–12.)

- *If those in heaven with the clearest view of reality are so exuberant and devoted in their worship of God, why don't we on earth catch a clue and adopt a similar approach?*
- *What, in your opinion, are the real reasons we aren't more worshipful of God?*
- *What are ways other than singing that we can worship?*

❼ **God doesn't *need* our worship.** God is complete, independent, and self-sufficient. It has been this way from eternity past and will ever remain so. Perfect and lacking nothing, he is in no way diminished if human creatures refuse or fail to worship. The heavens themselves shout the glory of God (Psalm 19:1), and he is surrounded by angelic beings who forever praise him (Revelation 4:8).

- *If God doesn't need our worship, why does he ask for it? Does this seem a bit vain to you?*

❽ **Worshiping God leads to ultimate fulfillment; worshiping anything other than God is idolatry.** "You will fill me with joy in your presence, with eternal pleasures at your right hand" (Psalm 16:11 NIV). "Delight yourself in the LORD and he will give you the desires of your heart" (Psalm 37:4 NIV). "You have made us for Yourself, O God, and our hearts are restless until they find their rest in You" (Augustine).

- *Most people view God as the ultimate party pooper and serving/worshiping God as a giant yawn. Yet the verses and statement above paint an opposite picture. How do you account for this contradiction?*
- *What are the implications of the statement that "we were created* by *God* for *God"?*

❾ **Worship involves a sense of the presence of God.** Whether it's bowing down *before* God (Psalm 95:2), seeking his face (Psalm 105:3–4), waiting *for* the Lord (Psalm 33:20–21), dwelling *in* his house (Psalm 84:4), lifting our hands (Psalm 134:2), or shouting *to* him (Psalm 47:1), worship always seems to involve a recognition that God is near.

- *Describe a time in your life when you were most aware of the presence of God.*
- *What do you try to do to "practice the presence of God" in your daily life?*

❿ **Worship should be active, emotional, and enjoyable.** The picture painted in Scripture is *not* of passive, sit-on-your-hands, dry, drab, going-through-the-motions worship. It is of enthusiastic celebration. The mood is one of gratitude and reverence, yet the worshipers seem genuinely excited (see 2 Samuel 6:13–15). They appear to be enjoying God as much as (possibly *more* than) any hunter enjoys the first day of deer season or a diligent student enjoys acing a test.

- *Do you* enjoy *worship? Look forward to it? Can you truly say worship is a* celebration *for you? Or is it a mere* ceremony? *Why?*
- *Imagine aliens secretly visiting a somber American church service and then an NFL play-off game. What would they conclude about each?*
- *What do you need to do differently as a result of this study on worship?*

Response *(6 minutes)*

Bring the group back together. Then ask: **"What did you learn? Anybody have a 'light bulb' go on above your head?"**

LEADER'S NOTES:

Leader's Notes:

Move quickly through this list, with individuals shouting out their specific examples.

Say: **"Okay, you've probably seen this verse before, but it's worth examining again. Let's conclude our time with a quick reflection on it: 'Whatever you eat or drink or *whatever you do*, you must do all for the glory of God'** (1 Corinthians 10:31 NLT; emphasis added).

"Let's brainstorm together just a couple of the following categories."
Have students give as many specific examples as they can for each category discussed.

Ask: **"What are some practical ways to . . . "**

***Sleep* for the glory of God?**

***Eat* for the glory of God?**

***Attend school* for the glory of God?**

***Work* for the glory of God?**

***Be a youth group member* for the glory of God?**

***Exercise* for the glory of God?**

***Drive* for the glory of God?**

***Play sports* for the glory of God?**

***Shop* for the glory of God?**

***Be a family member* for the glory of God?**

***Watch TV* for the glory of God?**

***Clean your room* for the glory of God?**

***Study* for the glory of God?**

***Go to the movies* for the glory of God?**

***Date* for the glory of God?**

Take everyone's suggestions and affirm them for their creative and spiritual thinking.

Wrap Up

Hand out INAM Weekly Devotions and encourage students to complete each day.

Close the session in prayer.

REPRODUCIBLE WORKSHEETS

for

Session 2

PEOPLE PANDEMONIUM

Instructions: As quickly and accurately as possible, accomplish each of the following items and secure required signature. You do not have to complete them in order.

❶ Find someone who has (or had) braces and get him or her to say "CHEESE!" while you pretend to take his or her picture. That person signs here:

❷ Get with two other people and do your best impersonation of supermodels walking down a runway during a fashion show (must walk all the way across the room). One of your threesome signs here:

❸ Find a partner and pretend to ride a bicycle built for two around the room—backward. Your cycling companion signs here:

❹ Try to breakdance or moonwalk and get a witness to sign here:

❺ Get the initials of someone who can imitate someone famous (Note: They must do their impersonation for you):

❻ Find someone who is smiling or laughing, introduce yourself, and get that person to sign here:

❼ Grab a partner, exchange names, then drop down and do fifteen push-ups or crunches. Stand back up and high-five each other. Sign each other's sheet here:

❽ Stand on a chair and give an impassioned 15-second speech on "How People Spend Their Precious Lives Doing Trivial Things." When you're finished, sign here:

God Is Glorious!

The heavens declare the glory of God. (Psalm 19:1 NIV)

Who among the gods is like you, O Lord? Who is like you—majestic in holiness, awesome in glory, working wonders? (Exodus 15:11 NIV)

Declare his glory among the nations, his marvelous deeds among all peoples.
(1 Chronicles 16:24 NIV)

God made all things, and everything continues through him and for him. To him be the glory forever. (Romans 11:36 NCV)

- Why do you think the Bible puts such an emphasis on the glory of God?

- What exactly is God's glory? How would you describe it? What kind of effect does the word "glory" produce in your mind?

- What does it mean to glorify God? How would you explain these concepts to a child? To an unbelieving friend?

God Is Glorious!

The heavens declare the glory of God. (Psalm 19:1 NIV)

Who among the gods is like you, O Lord? Who is like you—majestic in holiness, awesome in glory, working wonders? (Exodus 15:11 NIV)

Declare his glory among the nations, his marvelous deeds among all peoples.
(1 Chronicles 16:24 NIV)

God made all things, and everything continues through him and for him. To him be the glory forever. (Romans 11:36 NCV)

- Why do you think the Bible puts such an emphasis on the glory of God?

- What exactly is God's glory? How would you describe it? What kind of effect does the word "glory" produce in your mind?

- What does it mean to glorify God? How would you explain these concepts to a child? To an unbelieving friend?

Ten Transforming Truths about Worship

❶ **In its purest sense, worship is simply assigning worth or value to someone or something.** Why do we say this? Because the word *worship* actually derives from the Old English term *worthship* (the state of having worth or value).

- *What thoughts, words, and images come to mind when you think of the word* worship*?*
- *How would you define* worship *to an unchurched person who asked, "Why do you Christians sing about God every Sunday morning? What's up with that?"*

❷ **Worship involves the glad and lavish giving of our devotion.** That is, when we view someone or something as valuable, we eagerly devote our time, our allegiance, our affection, our emotional energy, our material resources, our praise to that person or thing.

- *Can you think of other specific ways people express their devotion?*
- *Why do we say that worship is "glad"? (Hint: Think of avid football fans or young couples in love.) Why do we say worship is "lavish"?*

❸ **Everyone in the world is a worshiper.** That is, we all have relationships or things in our lives we consider valuable and usually one person or thing we view as having supreme worth. It is not a question of "*Will* I worship?" but rather "*Who* or *what* will I worship?"

- *In what ways is this a new concept for you?*
- *Have you ever stopped to consider this idea before—that everyone on this planet worships someone or something?*

❹ **Not everyone in the world worships *God*.** (This statement shouldn't need any explanation!)

- *What, in your opinion, are the most common objects of worship among Americans?*
- *Now forget about relationships and objects. Think in terms of ideals (for example, comfort, pleasure, etc.). What are some other similar ideals to which many are devoted?*

❺ **What a person (truly) worships can be easily discovered.** That is, it's not hard to look at a person's life and tell what he or she values above all else. Look at his calendar or schedule book, listen to her conversation, and observe how he spends his money and emotions, and you will have a good indication of what the person considers to have the highest worth.

- *Why is it common for people to worship "self"?*
- *In what ways might people value "Christianity" more than "Christ"?*

❻ **The Bible speaks of God, our Creator and Redeemer, as the One who alone deserves our worship.** (Read Revelation 4:8–11; 7:9–12.)

- *If those in heaven with the clearest view of reality are so exuberant and devoted in their worship of God, why don't we on earth catch a clue and adopt a similar approach?*
- *What, in your opinion, are the real reasons we aren't more worshipful of God?*
- *What are ways other than singing that we can worship?*

❼ **God doesn't *need* our worship.** God is complete, independent, and self-sufficient. It has been this way from eternity past and will ever remain so. Perfect and lacking nothing, he is in no way diminished if human creatures refuse or fail to worship. The heavens themselves shout the glory of God (Psalm 19:1), and he is surrounded by angelic beings who forever praise him (Revelation 4:8).

- *If God doesn't need our worship, why does he ask for it? Does this seem a bit vain to you?*

❽ **Worshiping God leads to ultimate fulfillment; worshiping anything other than God is idolatry.** "You will fill me with joy in your presence, with eternal pleasures at your right hand" (Psalm 16:11 NIV). "Delight yourself in the LORD and he will give you the desires of your heart" (Psalm 37:4 NIV). "You have made us for Yourself, O God, and our hearts are restless until they find their rest in You" (Augustine).

- *Most people view God as the ultimate party pooper and serving/worshiping God as a giant yawn. Yet the verses and statement above paint an opposite picture. How do you account for this contradiction?*
- *What are the implications of the statement that "we were created* by *God* for *God"?*

❾ **Worship involves a sense of the presence of God.** Whether it's bowing down *before* God (Psalm 95:2), seeking his face (Psalm 105:3–4), waiting *for* the Lord (Psalm 33:20–21), dwelling *in* his house (Psalm 84:4), lifting our hands (Psalm 134:2), or shouting *to* him (Psalm 47:1), worship always seems to involve a recognition that God is near.

- *Describe a time in your life when you were most aware of the presence of God.*
- *What do you try to do to "practice the presence of God" in your daily life?*

❿ **Worship should be active, emotional, and enjoyable.** The picture painted in Scripture is *not* of passive, sit-on-your-hands, dry, drab, going-through-the-motions worship. It is of enthusiastic celebration. The mood is one of gratitude and reverence, yet the worshipers seem genuinely excited (see 2 Samuel 6:13–15). They appear to be enjoying God as much as (possibly *more* than) any hunter enjoys the first day of deer season or a diligent student enjoys acing a test.

- *Do you* enjoy *worship? Look forward to it? Can you truly say worship is a* celebration *for you? Or is it a mere* ceremony*? Why?*
- *Imagine aliens secretly visiting a somber American church service and then an NFL play-off game. What would they conclude about each?*
- *What do you need to do differently as a result of this study on worship?*

INAM WEEKLY DEVOTIONS

Day 1: God's Glorious Holiness

Seraphim stood above Him, each having six wings: with two he covered his face, and with two he covered his feet, and with two he flew.
And one called out to another and said,
"Holy, Holy, Holy, is the LORD of hosts,
The whole earth is full of His glory."
And the foundations of the thresholds trembled at the voice of him who called out, while the temple was filling with smoke.

Then I said,
"Woe is me, for I am ruined!
Because I am a man of unclean lips,
And I live among a people of unclean lips;
For my eyes have seen the King, the LORD of hosts." (Isaiah 6:2–5 NRSV)

Put yourself in Isaiah's place. Inject yourself into this scene. Then describe what you are thinking and feeling. What prompted the prophet to cry, "Woe is me, for I am ruined!"?

____

____

____

____

____

____

How would you explain the concept of God's holiness to a room full of fourth graders?

____

____

____

____

____

Day 2: God's Glorious Presence and Power

I am everywhere—both near and far, in heaven and on earth (Jeremiah 23:23–24 CEV).

O Sovereign LORD! You have made the heavens and earth by your great power. Nothing is too hard for you! (Jeremiah 32:17 NLT).

What is your reaction to the biblical claim that God is present everywhere? In what ways does this truth convict you today? Comfort you?

Someone has noted, "If you have a little god, you'll have big problems, but if you have a big God—the one true God—you'll have little problems." Is the God you serve and worship *big*? How awesome is he? If he's not, why not?

Day 3: God's Glorious Eternal Nature

God is great, and we do not know Him; nor can the number of His years be discovered (Job 36:26 NKJV).

You are from everlasting (Psalm 93:2 NKJV).

From eternity I am He (Isaiah 43:13 NASB).

In the space below try to put into words some of your own thoughts and feelings about the timelessness of God. What does it mean to you that God is eternal, without beginning or end?

Day 4: God's Glorious Consistency

I the L*ORD do not change (Malachi 3:6* NIV*).*

Jesus Christ is the same yesterday and today and forever (Hebrews 13:8 ESV*).*

Theologians refer to God's unchanging nature as his *immutability.* How is this quality a comfort (or how *could* it be reassuring) to someone facing uncertain times?

What advantages do you see in this divine truth?

Day 5: God's Glorious Love

Jesus told his followers: *"I have loved you even as the Father has loved me. Remain in my love" (John 15:9* NLT*).*

This is real love. It is not that we loved God, but that he loved us and sent his Son as a sacrifice to take away our sins (1 John 4:10 NLT*).*

When, if ever, did God's love become more than just a word or an idea? When did it become deeply personal and real to you?

Young Life® Adaptation for Session 2

Recommended for Wyldlife® Small Groups

This adaptation assumes a meeting designed primarily for enhancing relationships with students and for pre-evangelism. Note, however, that the main focus of Session 2 is God's glory. So you may have to work hard to keep fringe kids interested and involved.

Use the opener "People Pandemonium." This should be fun, especially with a large group.

Next, do the *Discussion* as presented and be sure to include the *Reading*.

For the *Bible Study Discussion* section, skip the "God Is Glorious" part, and begin after the first set of discussion questions, talking again about material in the *It's Not About Me, Teen Edition* book. Conclude this section with the *Dramas.*

Use the *Practical Application* section as written but be aware that it highlights worship. So go ahead and divide into groups, but if at all possible have an adult leader for each group to guide the discussion.

The *Response* should work well. After the discussion, thank them for their creative thinking and explain that you and the other staff will be happy to get together one-on-one to talk through any issues or questions they might have.

Recommended for Young Life Campaigners

This adaptation assumes a meeting designed for Young Life Senior High Campaigner groups. The attendees will be primarily new believers with little or no church background.

Begin with the *Reading* (7 minutes).

Follow with the *Bible Study Discussion* section as it is (10 minutes).

Next, go into the *Practical Application* (20 minutes), but don't break into groups and don't rush through this section.

Conclude with the *Response* section (8 minutes).

Remind everyone of the INAM Weekly Devotions.

living now with an eye on then

Primary Lesson Texts

Ecclesiastes 3:11
John 3:30
Romans 1:14–17
2 Corinthians 4:16–18

Lesson Focus/Key Concept

Because our lives and the people in our lives are quickly passing away, we need to invest ourselves in eternity. Our top priorities should be knowing and serving God and helping others do the same.

Lesson Goal

As a result of this lesson, students will be encouraged to begin living *this* day with *that* day (eternity) in view, and they will see the need to help prepare their friends for the life beyond this life.

Materials Needed

- ❑ Reproducible handouts, pages 54–61
- ❑ Pens/pencils
- ❑ Prize

LEADER'S NOTES:

Warmup/Openers *(10 minutes)*

Choose one of the following opener options.

❶ *Secret Desires*

Use this exercise to help students get better acquainted and also to subtly raise the issue of priorities (that is, how much an eternal perspective figures in students' values/mind-sets). Make copies of the "Secret Desires" reproducible sheet at the end of this session. Give one to each student.

Encourage everyone to be honest and anonymous. Also explain, however, that eventually the group will try to guess the owner of each "secret desire."

SECRET DESIRES!

In the space below, write out two or three of your wildest dreams (that you don't mind sharing with the group). For example, "I would like to play professional golf," "I would like to own a restaurant," "I would like to visit every country in the world," "I dream about having my whole family become serious followers of Christ." Then sign your name at the bottom, fold the paper, and hand it to your leader. He will read aloud your "Secret Desires," and the rest of the group will attempt to guess your identity.

1.

2.

3.

❷ *Useless Facts & Abilities*

This exercise, in addition to being potentially laugh-out-loud funny, calls to mind how absorbed we can become with information and activities that serve little or no eternal purpose.

Pick two or more competing teams (4–8 members each, depending on the size of your group) and another team of 3–5 judges. One at a time have members of each team step forward and demonstrate their odd "gifts" (for example, the ability to walk on one's hands, recite all the vowels while burping, do a great Elvis impression) or recite random true trivia (for example, "The lifetime goal for a guy in Texas is to visit and be photographed in front of every Starbucks in the world" or "The college freshman who spent every free minute competing in combat tournaments on the Internet ballooned to over 300 pounds from all the sitting and eating, and he now suffers from intestinal problems.")

Have the judges assign points 1–10 for each contestant based on the criteria of "originality, interest, creativity, and presentation." Add up the individual scores for each team. The team with the highest aggregate score is the "Useless!" championship team. Give them a prize.

Discussion *(10 minutes)*

Say: "**In previous generations, it was common to try to summarize a person's life or legacy on his or her cemetery headstone. Here are some such epitaphs (supposedly real, but some may be urban legends).**" Then read the following epitaphs:

In a Colorado cemetery:
He was young
He was fair
But the Injuns
Raised his hair

In a Uniontown, Pennsylvania, cemetery:
Here lies the body
of Jonathan Blake
Stepped on the gas
Instead of the brake.

Anna Hopewell's grave in Enosburg Falls, Vermont:
Here lies the body of our Anna
Done to death by a banana.
It wasn't the fruit that laid her low
But the skin of the thing that made her go.

In a London, England, cemetery:
Here lies Ann Mann,
Who lived an old maid
But died an old Mann.
Dec. 8, 1767

Then say: "**Now, understand I'm *not* trying to be morbid; however, I do want us to engage in some realistic thinking. The fact is, barring the return of Jesus, we *will* each die. So how do we make our lives count? How do we live here and now in such a way that we'll be ready for there and then (that is, heaven and eternity)? How do you live so that your epitaph is a little more substantive than some of the ones I've just read to you?**

"**Researchers tell us that the average North American with an average life span of approximately seventy-five years will spend:**

***about twenty-five years* sleeping**

***about fifteen years* working**

***some ten years* watching television**

***four years* eating**

Leader's Notes:

Be sensitive to those who recently may have experienced the death of a loved one.

Leader's Notes:

three years commuting/driving

three years in the bathroom

three years getting dressed"

Ask:

"Are you surprised by any of those figures?"

"What are some other time-consuming activities in your daily life?"

"How do you decide how to spend your time?"

"What shapes your priorities?"

"If life is all about God and not about us, and if we are here solely for his glory, how should we be spending our days?"

Say: **"These are hugely important questions because remember, how we spend our days is how we spend our lives!"**

Reading (5 minutes)

Choose these students beforehand, giving them time to read through their selections.

Have three students read the following excerpt, beginning on page 44 of *It's Not About Me, Teen Edition*, so that everyone has a better grasp of Max's explanation of the topic of eternal perspective. (Other students should follow along in their books.)

Reader #1:

Think back before people counted time. Before "moments." Is that what life in the Garden was like for Adam and Eve? Before the couple swallowed the line of Satan and the fruit of the tree, no one printed calendars or wore watches or needed cemeteries. They lived in a time-free world. But in the moment it takes to take a bite (of forbidden fruit), sin entered the world and with it, time. Our lives are a collection of moments, a measurable and countable supply, like change in a pocket or buttons in a can. Your pocket may be full of decades, my pocket may be down to a few years, but everyone has a certain number of moments.

Reader #2:

Everyone, that is, except God. As we list the mind-stretching claims of Christ, let's include this one near the top. "Before Abraham was born, I am." . . . Jesus claimed to be God, the Eternal Being. He identified himself as "the High and Lofty One Who inhabits eternity." . . .

Scripture broadcasts this attribute in surround-sound. God is "from everlasting" . . . and the "everlasting King" . . . "incorruptible" . . . "who alone has immortality." . . . The heavens and the earth will perish, "but You [O God] are the same, and Your years will have no end." . . . You'll more quickly measure the salt of the ocean than measure the existence of God because "the number of His years is unsearchable."

Reader #3:

Trace the tree back to a seed. Trace the dress back to a factory. Trace the baby back to a mommy. Trace God back to . . . to . . . to . . .

No one. Not even God made God. "From eternity I am He." . . . For that reason we have Jesus making statements such as, "Before Abraham was born, I am." . . . He didn't say, "Before Abraham was born, I was." God never says, "I was," because he still is. He is—right now—in the days of Abraham and in the end of time. He is eternal.

He does not live in sequential moments, laid out on a time line, one following the other. His world is one moment or, better stated, momentless.

He doesn't view history as a progression of centuries but as a single photo. He captures your life, your entire life, in one glance. He sees your birth and burial in one frame. He knows your beginning and your end, because he has neither.

Bible Study Discussion *(12 minutes)*

Make sure that every student has a copy of this reproducible Bible study discussion sheet. Read and discuss the passages as they are listed on the sheet, using the discussion questions included.

Living in Light of Eternity

Read and discuss the following Bible passages:

1. *"He has put eternity in their hearts" (Ecclesiastes 3:11 NKJV).*
   - What does it mean that God has "put eternity" in our hearts?
   - When in your life has heaven seemed most real and this world had its loosest grip on you?

2. The apostle Paul—a man who devoted his life to knowing Christ and making him known around the world (and who also suffered greatly for this cause) once wrote:

"Our light affliction, which is but for a moment, is working for us a far more exceeding and eternal weight of glory" (2 Corinthians 4:17 NKJV).

LEADER'S NOTES:

Move this along. Don't let the discussion drag.

Leader's Notes:

- Scholars estimate Paul served Christ faithfully for more than thirty *trial-filled* years. Why does Paul describe his affliction as "light" and "but for a moment?" Since when do 30+ years = "a moment"?

- How does a conscious awareness of eternity better equip us to live out our fleeting lives here and now? In other words, in what ways does the hope of heaven give us practical help for living on earth today?

- What long-term struggle are you having a difficult time enduring? What if you had to wrestle with that hardship for the rest of your life on earth? How does that prospect hit you?

- Now, think of the promise of eternity—problems traded for glory. How, if at all, does that divine assurance help you?

3. John the Baptist and the apostle Paul looked at life with eternity in mind.

John the Baptist (who was eventually killed for his faith) said: *"[Jesus] must become greater and greater, and I must become less and less" (John 3:30 NLT).*

The apostle Paul (who was eventually killed for his faith) said: *"I have a duty to all people" (Romans 1:14 NCV); "I am eager to come to you . . . to preach God's Good News" (Romans 1:15 NLT); "I am not ashamed of the gospel, because it is the power of God for the salvation of everyone who believes" (Romans 1:16 NIV).*

- Good news is for sharing. We almost never have to be prodded to tell others about exciting experiences or wonderful blessings; we do it naturally. Why do you think so many Christians are tight lipped about their faith, about the wonderful message of new life—*eternal* life—in Christ?

- If other Christians in the world imitated your exact practices and habits of "sharing the good news of Jesus," how effectively would the message be spreading?

- Name a few people you'd describe as God's messengers. Did you think of preachers and famous evangelists? The testimony of the Bible is that God uses all kinds of regular people, in all walks of life, to get his message across. In what specific ways do you sense God may be wanting to use you as a messenger today?

Conclude the discussion by reminding students, **"Paul existed to deliver the message. How people remembered him was secondary. How people remembered Christ was primary. Paul's message was not about himself. His message was all about Christ."**

Drama (5 minutes)

Before class, select two students to participate in the drama and give each one a copy of the reading below. Have the students alternate saying their lines. They each are espousing a world-view—the first, a secular, temporal mind-set; the second, a Christian, God-centered view. Make sure they read them creatively, with passion, and in a convincing manner.

Reader 1:	**Reader 2:**
My life is my life.	My life has been bought with a price—*Christ* is my life.
I want what I want.	I want what God wants.
Live for the moment.	Live for eternity.
Life is short—play hard.	Life is short—*pray* hard.
Mind your own business.	There's no such thing as your own business.
I am my own truth.	Jesus said, "*I* am . . . *the* truth."
Don't be so intolerant!	Good news is for sharing.
Christianity is too . . . confining.	You shall know the truth, and the truth shall set you free.
What do *you* know about freedom?	If the Son of Man sets you free, you are free indeed.
Nobody tells me what to do.	The one who sins is a slave to sin.
I have goals . . . and things I want.	What does it profit a person to gain the whole world and yet lose his or her own soul?
I have to be true to myself.	You must be born again.
Big deal if some guy died 2,000 years ago!	If Jesus Christ is God, and he died for me, no sacrifice can be too great for me to make for him.
Love things; use people.	Love people; use things.
I say, "*Protect* yourself."	Jesus said, "Give yourself away."
It's a crazy world. Be careful!	It's God's world. Lose your life for his sake.
You're a fool to live for God!	"He is no fool who gives what he cannot keep to gain what he cannot lose."
But what about *me*?	It's not about me or you . . . or us.
You'll regret your fanaticism one day.	One day I'll regret that I wasn't *more* radical about my faith.

Leader's Notes:

Have students rehearse this beforehand and read with passion.

LEADER'S NOTES:

But what about here and now?	What about there and then?
(Long pause)	
Do you think he'd accept me?	"Whosoever shall call upon the name of the Lord shall be saved."
(Long pause)	
It's all about him. It's all about *him*!	Amen and amen!

Practical Application *(15 minutes)*

Say: **"If our bottom-line premise in this INAM experiment is true—that is, if life is *not* about us—then it follows that our days and years on this earth should not be orchestrated around us. Maybe our great God has loftier reasons for putting us here. Maybe he wants us to use our time on earth for grander purposes than we could imagine."**

Divide into groups of four, and hand out copies of the reproducible sheet on page 57. Then read aloud the bold points of "Ten Foundational Truths."

TEN FOUNDATIONAL TRUTHS
(for developing an eternal perspective)

The word *remember* is found 166 times in the NIV translation of the Bible. In the book of Deuteronomy alone (Moses's farewell address to the nation of Israel), the word is found 16 times (along with numerous other commands to *not forget*).

Clearly there is great value in deliberately and regularly bringing to mind those things that are true. Sit down with a friend and spend some time reflecting on these ten indisputable, bedrock truths of the Christian faith.

❶ **We were created by God, for God. We exist solely to bring him glory.** *(Isaiah 43:7; Colossians 1:16)*

❷ **Life is extremely short.** *(Psalm 90:10–12; James 4:13–14)*

❸ **We live in an evil age.** *(Ephesians 5:15–16; Philippians 2:14–15)*

❹ **Heaven and hell are real places.** *(Philippians 3:20; Revelation 20:15)*

❺ **We can devote our time and attention either to temporal pursuits or to issues of eternal significance.** *(Matthew 6:33; 2 Corinthians 4:16–18)*

❻ **God calls Christians to be involved in evangelism and discipleship.** *(Matthew 4:19; 28:18–20; Acts 1:8)*

❼ We will one day stand before Christ and be evaluated for how we have lived our lives. *(2 Corinthians 5:9–11)*

❽ We have an enemy who wants to deceive, destroy, and devour us. *(John 8:44; Ephesians 6:10–13; 1 Peter 5:8)*

❾ We have a Creator and Savior who dearly loves us *(John 3:16; 1 John 4:10–11)* **and who has provided us with everything we need to live for him and serve him.** *(Galatians 5:16; 2 Peter 1:3)*

❿ We find real rewards and great joy only when we live wholeheartedly for God. *(Mark 10:29–30; John 15:10–11; Galatians 5:22–23; 2 Timothy 4:7–8)*

LEADER'S NOTES:

Response *(3 minutes)*

Have students spend a few minutes thinking about and discussing the end of their life on earth. They might wish to imagine their deathbed scene. Who is gathered there? What do they want to say and hear? How do they want to depart this life?

Next, tell each to imagine their future funeral service. How do they want to be remembered? What do they want their legacy to be? They should share their answers.

Finally, have each person share what epitaph he or she would want written on the tombstone.

Afterward, say: **"Epitaphs may sum up our lives. But in a very real sense, our lives now are also advertising our priorities and values. So consider the message your life is communicating to the world right now."**

Wrap Up

Follow by role-playing a few of the "Creative Ideas for Getting Friends to Talk about Issues of Eternal Significance" (see page 58). Take the first turn in leading a role-play, with one of the kids playing the "student." Then, depending on the maturity of your group, choose others to role-play in front of everyone, while you provide hands-on instruction.

Hand out INAM Weekly Devotions and encourage students to complete each day.

Conclude with prayer.

REPRODUCIBLE WORKSHEETS

for

Session 3

Secret Desires!

In the space below, write out two or three of your wildest dreams (that you don't mind sharing with the group). For example, "I would like to play professional golf," "I would like to own a restaurant," "I would like to visit every country in the world," "I dream about having my whole family become serious followers of Christ." Then sign your name at the bottom, fold the paper, and hand it to your leader. He will read aloud your "Secret Desires," and the rest of the group will attempt to guess your identity.

1.

2.

3.

Living in Light of Eternity

Read and discuss the following Bible passages:

❶ *"He has put eternity in their hearts" (Ecclesiastes 3:11 NKJV).*

- What does it mean that God has "put eternity" in our hearts?
- When in your life has heaven seemed most real and this world had its loosest grip on you?

❷ The apostle Paul—a man who devoted his life to knowing Christ and making him known around the world (and also a man who suffered greatly for this cause) once wrote:

"Our light affliction, which is but for a moment, is working for us a far more exceeding and eternal weight of glory" (2 Corinthians 4:17 NKJV).

- Scholars estimate Paul served Christ faithfully for more than thirty trial-filled years. Why does Paul describe his affliction as "light" and "but for a moment?" Since when do 30+ years = "a moment"?
- How does a conscious awareness of eternity better equip us to live out our fleeting lives here and now? In other words, in what ways does the hope of heaven give us practical help for living on earth today?
- What long-term struggle are you having a difficult time enduring? What if you had to wrestle with that hardship for the rest of your life on earth? How does that prospect hit you?
- Now, think of the promise of eternity—problems traded for glory. How, if at all, does that divine assurance help you?

❸ John the Baptist and the apostle Paul looked at life with eternity in mind.

John the Baptist (who was eventually killed for his faith) said: *"[Jesus] must become greater and greater, and I must become less and less" (John 3:30 NLT).*

The apostle Paul: *"I have a duty to all people" (Romans 1:14 NCV); "I am eager to come to you . . . to preach God's Good News" (Romans 1:15 NLT); "I am not ashamed of the gospel, because it is the power of God for the salvation of everyone who believes" (Romans 1:16 NIV).*

- Good news is for sharing. We almost never have to be prodded to tell others about exciting experiences or wonderful blessings; we do it naturally. Why do you think so many Christians are tight lipped about their faith, about the wonderful message of new life—*eternal* life—in Christ?
- If other Christians in the world imitated your exact practices and habits of "sharing the good news of Jesus," how effectively would the message be spreading?
- Name a few people you'd describe as God's messengers. Did you think of preachers and famous evangelists? The testimony of the Bible is that God uses all kinds of regular people, in all walks of life, to get his message across. In what specific ways do you sense God may want to use you as a messenger today?

Drama

Reader 1:	**Reader 2:**
My life is my life.	My life has been bought with a price—*Christ* is my life.
I want what I want.	I want what God wants.
Live for the moment.	Live for eternity.
Life is short—play hard.	Life is short—*pray* hard.
Mind your own business.	There's no such thing as your own business.
I am my own truth.	Jesus said, "*I* am . . . *the* truth."
Don't be so intolerant!	Good news is for sharing.
Christianity is too . . . confining.	You shall know the truth, and the truth shall set you free.
What do *you* know about freedom?	If the Son of Man sets you free, you are free indeed.
Nobody tells me what to do.	The one who sins is a slave to sin.
I have goals . . . and things I want.	What does it profit a person to gain the whole world and yet lose his or her own soul?
I have to be true to myself.	You must be born again.
Big deal if some guy died 2,000 years ago!	If Jesus Christ is God, and he died for me, no sacrifice can be too great for me to make for him.
Love things; use people.	Love people; use things.
I say, "*Protect* yourself."	Jesus said, "Give yourself away."
It's a crazy world. Be careful!	It's God's world. Lose your life for his sake.
You're a fool to live for God!	"He is no fool who gives what he cannot keep to gain what he cannot lose."
But what about *me*?	It's not about me or you . . . or us.
You'll regret your fanaticism one day.	One day I'll regret that I wasn't *more* radical about my faith.
But what about here and now?	What about there and then?

(Long pause)

Do you think he'd accept me?	"Whosoever shall call upon the name of the Lord shall be saved."

(Long pause)

It's all about him. It's all about *him*!	Amen and amen!

TEN FOUNDATIONAL TRUTHS

(for developing an eternal perspective)

The word *remember* is found 166 times in the NIV translation of the Bible. In the book of Deuteronomy alone (Moses's farewell address to the nation of Israel), the word is found 16 times (along with numerous other commands to *not forget*).

Clearly there is great value in deliberately and regularly bringing to mind those things that are true. Sit down with a friend and spend some time reflecting on these ten indisputable, bedrock truths of the Christian faith:

❶ **We were created by God, for God. We exist solely to bring him glory.** *(Isaiah 43:7; Colossians 1:16)*

❷ **Life is extremely short.** *(Psalm 90:10–12; James 4:13–14)*

❸ **We live in an evil age.** *(Ephesians 5:15–16; Philippians 2:14–15)*

❹ **Heaven and hell are real places.** *(Philippians 3:20; Revelation 20:15)*

❺ **We can devote our time and attention either to temporal pursuits or to issues of eternal significance.** *(Matthew 6:33; 2 Corinthians 4:16–18)*

❻ **God calls Christians to be involved in evangelism and discipleship.** *(Matthew 4:19; 28:18–20; Acts 1:8)*

❼ **We will one day stand before Christ and be evaluated for how we have lived our lives.** *(2 Corinthians 5:9–11)*

❽ **We have an enemy who wants to deceive, destroy, and devour us.** *(John 8:44; Ephesians 6:10–13; 1 Peter 5:8)*

❾ **We have a Creator and Savior who dearly loves us** *(John 3:16; 1 John 4:10–11)* **and who has provided us with everything we need to live for him and serve him.** *(Galatians 5:16; 2 Peter 1:3)*

❿ **We find real rewards and great joy only when we live wholeheartedly for God.** *(Mark 10:29–30; John 15:10–11; Galatians 5:22–23; 2 Timothy 4:7–8)*

Creative Ideas for Getting Friends to Talk about Issues of Eternal Significance

❶ Do you ever think about heaven? How do you think a person gets there? Would you be interested in what the Bible says?

❷ Ask about religious/church background:
- What do you think about your church experience (if any) from your childhood?
- Do you take your religious beliefs *more* seriously or *less* seriously than when you were younger?

❸ What are your goals in life? Do you have *spiritual* goals?

❹ What do you think is the biggest problem most people face? What's the solution to that problem? What role, if any, do you think God/Christ might play in solving that problem?

❺ In your opinion, how does one become a Christian? Would you be interested in seeing what the Bible says on this subject?

❻ What's the first thing that comes to mind when you hear the word *Christianity*?

❼ You know, we've been friends for a long time, and yet I've never really told you about the most important thing in my life. Could I tell you about that right now?

❽ Do you ever pray? When? [Typical answer: "Usually when I'm in trouble."] Do you ever feel like your prayers are just bouncing off the ceiling? I had the same experience until someone shared with me how to know God in a deeply personal way. Would you be interested in what that person told me?

❾ Do you ever go to church? Does it do much for you? [Usually not.] You know, I felt the same way until someone explained to me the difference between *religion* and a *relationship with God*. Have you ever considered the difference between those two things?

❿ Has anyone ever shown you from the Bible how you can know *for sure* that you're going to heaven? May I?

⓫ If you died tonight, do you know *for sure* where you would spend eternity? Would you like to know?

⓬ If you died and God asked, "Why should I let you into heaven?" what would you say?

⓭ What do you think happens after we die? Would you like to see what the Bible says about that subject?

⓮ [After a Christian event in which the gospel is presented, you can ask this] So, what do you think? Did it make sense? Have you ever trusted in Christ like the speaker talked about? Really! When? Tell me about it. [If the person's response is vague you could go to questions 11 or 12.]

⓯ Did you know there is someone in the Bible just like you? [Depending on their situation, go to: the social outcast (Zacchaeus in Luke 19); the person in a shameful situation (the adulterous woman in John 8); the highly religious yet empty person (Nicodemus in John 3); the party person who has hit rock bottom (the Prodigal Son in Luke 15); the person in crisis (the royal official in John 4); the disillusioned person (the woman at the well in John 4).]

⓰ What do you think about Easter? Have you ever considered the significance of Christ's having risen from the dead?

⓱ If someone reports negative experiences with religion, say, "You're not alone! I've experienced a lot of those same things. And you know what? Even Jesus Christ had his run-ins with the religious establishment! Maybe that's why I find him so interesting and appealing. His perspective on relating to God is really refreshing!"

⓲ You know, I think in one way or another, we're all on a kind of spiritual journey. Where would you say you are in your quest to find meaning and purpose in life?

INAM WEEKLY DEVOTIONS

Day 1

Then Jesus told this story to some who had great self-confidence and scorned everyone else: "Two men went to the Temple to pray. One was a Pharisee, and the other was a dishonest tax collector. The proud Pharisee stood by himself and prayed this prayer: 'I thank you, God, that I am not a sinner like everyone else, especially like that tax collector over there! For I never cheat, I don't sin, I don't commit adultery, I fast twice a week, and I give you a tenth of my income.' But the tax collector stood at a distance and dared not even lift his eyes to heaven as he prayed. Instead, he beat his chest in sorrow, saying, 'O God, be merciful to me, for I am a sinner.' I tell you, this sinner, not the Pharisee, returned home justified before God. For the proud will be humbled, but the humble will be honored" (Luke 18:9–14 NLT).

▶ What is the main lesson Jesus is teaching here?

____

____

____

____

____

____

▶ In what way does this passage suggest that salvation (being made right with God) is "all about God"?

____

____

____

____

____

____

____

Day 2

So our aim is to please him always, whether we are here in this body or away from this body. For we must all stand before Christ to be judged. We will each receive whatever we deserve for the good or evil we have done in our bodies (2 Corinthians 5:9–10 NLT).

How would it change your life today if you could live with a constant awareness that one day you will stand before Jesus and give an account for the way you've lived your life?

____

____

____

____

____

Day 3

So be careful how you live, not as fools but as those who are wise. Make the most of every opportunity for doing good in these evil days. Don't act thoughtlessly, but try to understand what the Lord wants you to do (Ephesians 5:15–17 NLT).

Pull out your calendar or appointment book. Look over your "to-do" list for yesterday or tomorrow. What jumps out at you? What do you see? What does your use of time reveal about your priorities and what you believe?

____

____

____

____

____

Are your plans wise? Do they reflect what the Lord wants you to do? Most important, where is God in all your plans?

____

____

____

____

____

Day 4

But when the Holy Spirit has come upon you, you will receive power and will tell people about me [Jesus] everywhere (Acts 1:8 NLT).

Examine this verse carefully. What does it promise? Command?

Now hold your life up against that verse. Are you devoting your life to making sure the message of eternal life in Christ gets to the ends of the earth? How can you do that more effectively today?

Day 5

Let your light shine before men, that they may see your good deeds and praise your Father in heaven (Matthew 5:16 NIV).

Think about your life during the last week—your actions, your words, and your encounters with others. In what ways did you "shine"?

How have you pointed people to God?

Young Life® Adaptation for Session 3

Recommended for Wyldlife® Small Groups

This adaptation assumes a meeting designed primarily for enhancing relationships with students and for pre-evangelism. Because this session highlights the importance of sharing one's faith, you may have to work a bit harder at keeping non-Christian students engaged.

Use either opening activity—"Secret Desires!" or "Useless Facts & Abilities."

Next, do the *Discussion* as presented.

Don't let *Reading* drag. Be sure to choose students who can read well—clearly and with energy. You may want to edit this down a bit because it is long.

For *Bible Study Discussion*, don't hand out the discussion sheets. Instead, lead the group in a discussion (using the questions on the sheet) of Ecclesiastes 3:11 and then 2 Corinthians 4:17. Then move directly into the *Drama.*

For *Practical Application,* go ahead and divide into groups of four, but try to have an adult leader in each group to lead the discussion. Read the "Ten Foundational Truths" and do the epitaph exercise, but don't do the "Creative Ideas for Getting Friends to Talk" role-play.

Then, either (1) pull everyone back together, thank them for coming, mention that you and the other staff would be happy to talk with anyone about this session's topic, and close in prayer; *or* (2) have the adult leaders from the groups offer to talk with students individually and close their groups in prayer.

Recommended for Young Life Campaigners

This adaptation assumes a meeting designed for Young Life Senior High Campaigner groups. The attendees will be primarily new believers with little or no church background.

Begin with *Discussion* (10 minutes).

Go directly into *Reading* (5 minutes).

Follow this with *Bible Study Discussion* (10 minutes).

Conclude with *Practical Application* and *Response* (20 minutes).

Remind everyone of the INAM Weekly Devotions.

session 4

body business

Primary Lesson Texts

1 Corinthians 6:12, 15, 18–20
Romans 6:13

Lesson Focus/Key Concept

Because your body is God's *tool*, you must maintain it. Because your body is God's *temple*, you must respect it.

Lesson Goal

As a result of this lesson, students will realize their bodies belong totally to God, and they will be motivated to use their bodies to bring the Lord glory and honor.

Materials Needed

- ❑ Reproducible handouts, pages 73–80
- ❑ Pens/pencils
- ❑ Paper
- ❑ Prize

LEADER'S NOTES:

Also explain that students may not sign their own sheets.

Warmup/Opener (10 minutes)

Body Basics

Use this mixer with any size group to encourage group members to laugh a bit, mix and mingle, find out a few basic facts about each other, and to introduce the topic of "body." Play until someone completes the sheet or until five minutes are up. Award a prize to the winner.

Here's how it works:

1. Give everyone a copy of the game sheet below. (Copy the reproducible sheet on page 73.)
2. Instruct everyone to move about the room and get signatures by each of the statements below.
3. A person may sign next to a statement only if that statement is true of him or her.
4. Each person may sign another's sheet only once.
5. The first person to get a signature by each statement wins.

BODY BASICS

Quickly move about the room and find individuals who can truthfully sign by each of the following descriptions. Note: You may not let the same person sign more than once!

- I have blue eyes:
- I have a dimple (must show):
- I am over six feet tall:
- I have dieted/watched my weight/counted calories in the last year:
- I have ridden an exercise bike in the last year:
- I enjoy watching bodybuilding competitions on television:
- I have run at least five miles in the last week:
- I have a birthmark:
- I am double-jointed:
- I work on my tan whenever possible:
- I own some kind of exercise equipment (home gym, treadmill):
- I can wiggle my ears (demonstrate):
- I have monkey toes (second toe longer than big toe):
- My hair is longer than my mom would like:

After determining the winner, see who signed some of the more unusual statements (for example, bullets 6–14).

Discussion *(10 minutes)*

Agree — Disagree

Use this revealing exercise to let students see where they and their peers stand on certain "controversial" issues regarding our bodies. You may want to utilize this discussion starter with a big group (and have them raise hands, stand up, or move to one side of the room or the other), but peer pressure can sometimes prevent people from answering honestly. To encourage honesty, have your group sit in a circle, distribute the reproducible "agree" and "disagree" signs, making sure that each person has one of each. Then explain that immediately after you read a statement, everyone in the group should hold up the appropriate sign at the same time. Continue until you have worked through all the statements below.

This exercise always prompts plenty of debate and lends itself to natural follow-up questions (for example, "Those of you who said, 'disagree,' why do you feel that way?"). Definitely preface this exercise with some words about trying to understand other points of view and resisting the urge to judge or argue.

Watch your time. With discussion, this exercise could easily eat up 45 minutes or more!

Read the following issues:

- **A committed Christian will not get a tattoo.**
- **Christians should always dress in the latest fashions.**
- **It is hypocritical to penalize the tobacco companies for the serious health problems their products cause and not to penalize makers of junk food.**
- **Bodybuilding competitions are sick and weird.**
- **Most professional athletes are disgusting.**
- **Schools should require kids to participate in P.E. every day.**
- **Something is deeply wrong when the average American teenager spends more each year on hair care than most entire families in third world countries earn in a year.**
- **There's nothing wrong with eating junk food.**
- **Plastic surgery is vain and superficial and, in most cases, wrong.**
- **The Bible takes a somewhat disapproving view of sex.**

Afterward, thank the group for being honest. Then explain that if they haven't already figured it out, the focus of this session is our bodies.

LEADER'S NOTES:

Resist the urge to comment on individual students' responses. After each response, move quickly to the next statement.

LEADER'S NOTES:

Bible Study Discussion (15 minutes)

Read aloud the following section from chapter 11 of *It's Not About Me, Teen Edition* (p. 104). Have students follow along in their books.

Say: **"Our culture has a serious problem with sex. There is far too much focus on sex and the body as a plaything instead of the temple of God. But we are not the first culture with this problem."**

When it comes to our bodies, the Bible declares that we don't own them. "You are no longer your own. God paid a great price for you. So use your body to honor God" (1 Corinthians 6:19–20 CEV).

Use your body to indulge your passions? To grab attention? To express your opinions? No. Use your body to honor God. "Use your whole body as a tool to do what is right for the glory of God" (Romans 6:13 NLT). Your body is God's instrument, intended for his work and for his glory.

The Corinthian Christians had serious trouble with this. When it came to the body, they insisted, "We can do anything we want to" (1 Corinthians 6:12 CEV). Their philosophy conveniently separated flesh from spirit. Have fun with the flesh. Honor God with the spirit. Wild Saturdays. Worshipful Sundays. You can have it all. Sound familiar?

Paul disagreed. He reminded his readers that God interwove body with soul, elevating them to equal status. Your body is no toy. Quite the contrary. Your body is a tool. "Do you not know that your bodies are members of Christ himself?" (1 Corinthians 6:15 NIV).

What work is more important than God's? Doesn't it stand to reason that God's tools should be maintained? . . . Maintain God's instrument. Feed it. Rest it. When he needs a sturdy implement—a servant who is rested enough to serve, fueled enough to work, alert enough to think—let him find one in you. He uses you.

Greater still, he lives in you. "Don't you know that your body is the temple of the Holy Spirit, who lives in you?" (1 Corinthians 6:19 NLT). Paul wrote these words to counter the Corinthian sex obsession. "Run away from sexual sin!" reads the prior sentence. "No other sin so clearly affects the body as this one does. For sexual immorality is a sin against your own body. . ." (1 Corinthians 6:18 NLT).

You know the sexual anthem of our day: "I'll do what I want. It's my body." God's firm response? "No, it's not. It's mine."

Afterward, say: **"Would you agree that our twenty-first-century Western culture is body-obsessed? Consider how many billions of dollars are spent annually by those who want . . ."**

- **a *smaller* body** (ask the group for specific examples of this—for example, weight-loss plans, diet pills, low-fat or low-carb foods)
- **a *new/different* body** (ask for specific examples of this—for example, the mushrooming plastic surgery phenomenon)
- **a more *toned* or *muscular* body** (ask for specific examples of this—for example, health clubs, home gyms, other exercise equipment, the proliferation of steroid use)
- **to gawk at *naked* bodies** (ask for specific examples of this—for example, the exploding pornography plague. Note: According to Family Safe Media, kids in the age group of 12- to 17-year-olds are the heaviest viewers of Internet pornography.)
- **to *decorate* their bodies** (ask for specific examples of this—for example, hair care, nail care, skin care, fashion, and makeup, tattooing, body piercing, and so forth. There is the growing problem of girls showing off their bodies—even Christian girls—wearing the latest fashionable clothing of spaghetti-strap tanks; cropped tops and short shorts; low-cut tight tops; tiny T-shirts and low-rider jeans; gym shorts with sexy messages emblazoned across the seat. It's tough enough for a guy to worship any time, much less when he looks one way at youth group and sees a girl's sexy, flat tummy, and another direction and sees another girl's thong underwear visible above her hip-hugging jeans.)

Ask:

"What do you make of these trends?"

"What does this obsession with our bodies say about us as a culture?"

Practical Application *(10 minutes)*

Explain that you want to take a few minutes to look more carefully at the Bible passages cited by Max Lucado in the *It's Not About Me, Teen Edition* book.

Break into smaller groups. Assign a "leader" for each group. This doesn't have to be an adult. Give each student a copy of the following handout—a reproducible version is found at the end of the session. Explain that they should take a few minutes to answer the questions privately and honestly; then discuss them.

LEADER'S NOTES:

Be sensitive to any kids in the room who fit this description. In other words, don't single them out.

Make sure that the student leaders you choose can lead a group through this discussion.

Leader's Notes:

Heavenly Bodies

Using Our Bodies for the Glory of God

In chapter 11 Max writes of the attitudes and practices of the first-century Corinthian Christians:

> *When it came to the body, they insisted, "We can do anything we want to" (1 Corinthians 6:12 CEV). Their philosophy conveniently separated flesh from spirit. Have fun with the flesh. Honor God with the spirit. Wild Saturdays. Worshipful Sundays. You can have it all.*

- How prevalent is this mind-set today among teenagers who claim to be followers of Jesus? Why do you think this is true?

"You are no longer your own. God paid a great price for you. So use your body to honor God." (1 Corinthians 6:19–20 CEV)

- What sacrifice does this passage show?
- According to this passage, who holds the title deed to our lives?
- If we really believed this today, in what ways would we alter our activities?

"Use your whole body as a tool to do what is right for the glory of God."
(Romans 6:13 NLT)

- What does it mean to use one's body as a tool for God?
- What are some specific ways a person can do this?

"Don't you know that your body is the temple of the Holy Spirit, who lives in you?" (1 Corinthians 6:19 NLT)

- What are the implications of this verse—that the Spirit of God lives *in* us?
- Why don't we work that hard to make ourselves—our lives, our hearts, and our bodies—a fit home for Christ?
- According to this passage, what kind of person does God use?

Hand out the reproducible work sheet "Reflection Questions" to students who may want to think further about this.

"Run away from sexual sin! No other sin so clearly affects the body as this one does. For sexual immorality is a sin against your own body." (1 Corinthians 6:18 NLT)

- How is it that sexual sin affects the body more than other kinds of sin?

- What would you say to the common claim that, "Sex is no big deal; it's just a physical act"?
- Is God antisex? How do you know? Why do you think God made sexual intimacy feel so amazing?

Leader's Notes:

Be sure to choose students who can pull this off.

Drama (5 minutes)

These silent dramas can use up to 10–12 students, depending on the size of your group. They will need at least a few minutes to confer and plan before attempting.

Against the Flow

The idea is to convey (seriously, not humorously) without any dialogue the dilemma and hardship of going against the flow of culture in keeping oneself pure and using one's body to honor God.

The setup is a steady parade of characters moving in one direction, all of them trying to entice the protagonist to turn and go with them. He or she, deeply tempted and with great difficulty, tries to move in the opposite direction. At the end, another person joins him or her to journey in the same, God-honoring direction. Now, as a couple, they are visibly strengthened.

Here are some possible situations to use:

- the group encouraging drinking
- the group encouraging drug use
- the group encouraging sexual involvement
- the group *discouraging* positive uses of the body—exercise (running the race), service, efforts to put off certain sins

Afterward, ask:

- **"When have you felt alone in trying to honor God with your body?"**
- **"In what ways is it most difficult for you to maintain and respect your body every day?"**
- **"Why do temptations vary from person to person?"**
- **"How can friends make a difference in helping us to live rightly?"**

Ensure each group leader has paper and a pen

Response (10 minutes)

Divide back into groups and have students brainstorm responses to the following items. Have one person in each group keep track of their answers.

LEADER'S NOTES:

Move in and out of groups quickly.

❶ List ten wrong things people do with their physical bodies.

❷ List ten good, God-honoring things you can do with your physical bodies this next week.

Wrap Up

Ask each group to close in prayer, committing these truths and desires to the Lord.

Hand out INAM Weekly Devotions and encourage students to complete each day.

Offer to meet with any student who wants to discuss this more in depth. Reproducible Reflection Questions are included in the Reproducible Worksheets.

REPRODUCIBLE WORKSHEETS

for

Session 4

BODY BASICS

Quickly move about the room and find individuals who can truthfully sign or initial by each of the following descriptions. NOTE: You cannot let the same person sign more than once and you cannot sign your own sheet:

Signature:

- I have blue eyes: ____________________
- I have a dimple (must show): ____________________
- I am over six feet tall: ____________________
- I have dieted/watched my weight/counted calories in the last year: ____________________
- I have ridden an exercise bike in the last year: ____________________
- I enjoy watching bodybuilding competitions on television: ____________________
- I have run at least five miles in the last week: ____________________
- I have a birthmark: ____________________
- I am double-jointed: ____________________
- I work on my tan whenever possible: ____________________
- I own some kind of exercise equipment (home gym, treadmill): ____________________
- I can wiggle my ears (demonstrate): ____________________
- I have monkey toes (second toe longer than big toe): ____________________
- My hair is longer than my mom would like: ____________________

AGREE — DISAGREE

AGREE

DISAGREE

Heavenly Bodies

Using Our Bodies for the Glory of God

In chapter 11 Max writes of the attitudes and practices of the first-century Corinthian Christians:

> *When it came to the body, they insisted, "We can do anything we want to" (1 Corinthians 6:12* CEV*). Their philosophy conveniently separated flesh from spirit. Have fun with the flesh. Honor God with the spirit. Wild Saturdays. Worshipful Sundays. You can have it all.*

- How prevalent is this mind-set today among teenagers who claim to be followers of Jesus? Why do you think this is true?

"You are no longer your own. God paid a great price for you. So use your body to honor God" (1 Corinthians 6:19–20 CEV*).*

- What sacrifice does this passage show?

- According to this passage, who holds the title deed to our lives?

- If we really believed this today, in what ways would we alter our activities?

"Use your whole body as a tool to do what is right for the glory of God." (Romans 6:13 NLT*)*

- What does it mean to use one's body as a tool for God?

- What are some specific ways a person can do this?

"Don't you know that your body is the temple of the Holy Spirit, who lives in you?" (1 Corinthians 6:19 NLT)

- What are the implications of this verse—that the Spirit of God lives *in* us?

- Why don't we work that hard to make ourselves—our lives, our hearts, and our bodies—a fit home for Christ?

- According to this passage, what kind of person does God use?

"Run away from sexual sin! No other sin so clearly affects the body as this one does. For sexual immorality is a sin against your own body." (1 Corinthians 6:18 NLT)

- How is it that sexual sin affects the body more than other kinds of sin?

- What would you say to the common claim that, "Sex is no big deal; it's just a physical act"?

- Is God antisex? How do you know? Why do you think God made sexual intimacy feel so amazing?

REFLECTION QUESTIONS

(for individual use or discussion in accountability partnerships)

In your personal devotional time or with a friend this week, bounce around these questions:

- *How much value do you put on how your body looks?*

- *Why do some kids take meticulous care of their vehicles or rooms or clothes or computers and give little or no thought to the careful maintenance of their bodies?*

- *On a scale of 1–10, with 1 = "Gone to the dogs" and 10 = "A finely tuned instrument," how well are you currently taking care of your body?*

- *Contrast the behavior that might accompany the belief, "My body is mine, so I can do whatever I want with it" with the likely actions of the person who believes, "Since God owns my body, I will use it to honor him."*

- *What do you sense God is saying to you in this lesson about how to view your body?*

- *What steps can you take to better use your body for God and his purposes?*

INAM WEEKLY DEVOTIONS

Day 1

In a wealthy home some utensils are made of gold and silver, and some are made of wood and clay. The expensive utensils are used for special occasions, and the cheap ones are for everyday use. If you keep yourself pure, you will be a utensil God can use for his purpose. Your life will be clean, and you will be ready for the Master to use you for every good work (2 Timothy 2:20–21 NLT).

- What does it mean that we are God's "utensils"?

____

____

____

- How do you think God wants to use you (see Ephesians 2:10)? What in your life might be keeping him from using you more powerfully?

____

____

____

Day 2

Workouts in the gymnasium are useful, but a disciplined life in God is far more so, making you fit both today and forever (1 Timothy 4:8 MSG).

- What did the apostle Paul mean when he wrote this?

____

____

____

- It's obviously not good for us to let our bodies go, but what about the opposite extreme—what about fitness fanatics who spend countless hours each week engaging in physical exercise? Is this what God wants? How do we know where to draw the line?

____

____

____

Day 3

Jesus is speaking: *"And I will pray the Father, and He will give you another Helper, that He may abide with you forever" (John 14:16 NKJV).*

In speaking of "another Helper," Jesus was referring to the Holy Spirit, who, beginning at Pentecost, would indwell all Christians. That's what *abide* means: to indwell, to live in, to settle down and make oneself at home. In past generations people spoke of the house in which they resided as their "abode." It's the same root word. To abide in a place means to make that place your abode. In short, Jesus was saying, "In the person of the Holy Spirit, I'm going to make my home inside each and every person who believes in me."

- How does it make you feel to realize that your heart could be the dwelling place of Jesus Christ?

____

____

____

____

- Look at it this way—if you found out that an important dignitary was coming to stay at your home, what would you do to get ready?

____

____

____

____

____

Day 4

God owns the whole works. So let people see God in and through your body (1 Corinthians 6:20 MSG).

- When outsiders look at how you maintain your body and what you use it for, are they attracted to God or repelled?

____

____

____

____

____

Day 5

Run away from sexual sin! (1 Corinthians 6:18 NLT).

- What does running from sexual sin look like in your life?

- What are some specific ways you could avoid sexual temptation and say no to sensual urges?

Young Life® Adaptation for Session 4

Recommended for Wyldlife® Small Groups

This adaptation assumes a meeting designed primarily for enhancing relationships with students and for pre-evangelism. Students should be able to identify with the focus of this session (the body) because pop culture emphasizes beauty, image, sports, and sex. So you should have no trouble getting discussion going.

Use the opener "Body Basics." This should be fun, especially with a large group.

The "Agree – Disagree" exercise in the *Discussion* section should work well. Be careful not to get off on a tangent discussing some of the statements.

The reading at the beginning of the *Bible Study Discussion* section is a bit long. Instead of having it read aloud, summarize the housesitting illustration found in *It's Not About Me, Teen Edition,* page 104. Then read aloud part of the Max quote, beginning with "When it comes to our bodies . . ." and ending with "Doesn't it stand to reason that God's tools should be maintained?" The discussion that follows should work well.

Next, skip the "Heavenly Bodies" worksheet; instead, have selected students perform the "Against the Flow" dramas.

Then skip the *Practical Application* section and move directly to *Response.*

Close with a corporate prayer and offer for the adult leaders to meet with any students individually.

Recommended for Young Life Campaigners

This adaptation assumes a meeting designed for Young Life Senior High Campaigner groups. The attendees will be primarily new believers with little or no church background.

Begin with *Discussion* (10 minutes), using the "Agree–Disagree" signs.

Next, work through the *Bible Study Discussion* section (15 minutes).

Follow with *Practical Application* (10 minutes), but don't feel obligated to break into groups. Conclude with *Response* (10 minutes).

Remind everyone of the INAM Weekly Devotions.

session 5

when life stinks

Primary Lesson Texts

Psalm 103:8–11
Psalm 50:15
John 9:1–3

Lesson Focus/Key Concept

Your pain has a purpose. Your problems, struggles, heartaches, and hassles cooperate toward one end—the glory of God.

Lesson Goal

As a result of this lesson, students will understand that even in life's worst moments (and perhaps especially then), they can bring God great honor.

Materials Needed

- ❑ Reproducible handouts, pages 93–99
- ❑ Pens/pencils
- ❑ Index cards
- ❑ Prize

LEADER'S NOTES:

Also mention that students may not sign their own sheets.

Warmup/Openers (10 minutes)

Choose one of the following openers.

❶ Bummer Bingo

Use this mixer with any size group to encourage folks to meet, find out a few basic facts about each other, and to introduce the topic of trouble and hardship.

Give each student a copy of the "Bummer Bingo" game (see reproducible pages following this session). The goal is to get five signatures in a row, either across, up and down, or diagonally. A person may sign a box only if that statement is true of him or her. Each person may sign another's sheet only once.

Whoever gets five signatures in a row and first yells "BUMMER!" wins. Award a prize to the winner.

BUMMER BINGO

I have had a broken bone.	I have been dumped.	I have spent at least one night in a hospital.	My parents are separated or divorced.	I have had a friend or loved one die.
Someone in my family has/had cancer.	I have been fired from a job.	I have had stomach crud in the last six months.	I am allergic to some kind of food.	I have to take medication regularly.
I have been cut from a team.	I have failed a test in the last few weeks.	My best friend has moved away.	I have been robbed.	I have gotten detention at school.
I have been in a wreck.	I have had mono.	I can't see a thing without my glasses.	My house has flooded or had a fire.	One or both of my parents got laid off.
Bad Thing of your choice.	I have a disability.	I have suffered a season-ending injury.	I have been admitted to an ER in the last year.	I have moved more than three times in my life.

❷ Scenarios

Use this informative mixer to give people an opportunity to find out little-known facts about each other and to raise the issue of responding to difficulty.

Leader's Notes:

SCENARIOS

Break into groups of four, pass out sheets (see reproducible page), then take seven minutes to answer the following questions. Begin with "the person who has broken the most bones in his or her body." Proceed clockwise with each person answering one question, until time runs out or each person has answered all of the questions. Be honest!

- What would you do if . . . you were in a convenience store and a masked gunman suddenly came in to rob the place?
- What would you do if . . . someone broke a date with you to go out with one of your closest friends?
- What would you do if . . . your car broke down in the worst part of town at night—and your cell phone was dead?
- What would you do if . . . your house or apartment burned down and everything you owned was gone?
- What would you do if . . . our entire economy collapsed and we found ourselves in the middle of Great Depression II?
- What would you do if . . . you wrecked a friend's car that you weren't even supposed to be driving?
- What would you do if . . . your parent(s) announced you were moving 1,000 miles away—in 30 days?
- What would you do if . . . you discovered you had a debilitating or deadly illness (e.g., AIDS, cystic fibrosis, leukemia, ALS, cancer)?

Afterward, discuss the experience.

Discussion (5 minutes)

To introduce this, say: **"We've all heard of the famous Murphy's Law—'Anything that can go wrong will go wrong.' Did you know there are numerous elaborations of this general principle and related rules? For example:"**

- **If anything simply cannot go wrong, it will anyway.**
- **If there is a possibility of several things going wrong, the one that will cause the most damage will be the one to go wrong.**
- **If you determine that there are four possible ways in which a procedure can go**

LEADER'S NOTES:

If you can put these into a PowerPoint presentation, your group will have a visual way to track with you.

wrong, and you manage to circumvent these, then a fifth way, unprepared for, will promptly develop.

- **If everything seems to be going well, you have obviously overlooked something.**
- **It is impossible to make anything foolproof because fools are so ingenious.**
- **Every solution breeds new problems.**
- **Nothing is as easy as it looks.**
- **Everything takes longer than you think.**

Ask what Murphy's Law experiences they've had, and let some kids share their stories.

Reading (5 minutes)

Read aloud these first few paragraphs of chapter 12 of *It's Not About Me, Teen Edition* (p. 114). This will be helpful to those students who either do not have the book or who did not read the book.

> *Nika, a vibrant eighteen-year-old Christian, was voted Most Likely to Succeed in high school and headed off to college to pursue her dream of replacing Diane Sawyer on* Prime Time Live. *There she wrote for the school newspaper and volunteered at the campus radio station. She joined a social club (similar to a sorority), went to church, waited tables at an Italian restaurant, spent time with her boyfriend, and juggled all this while taking eighteen hours of coursework. Life was full—and full of promise.*
>
> *Six weeks after her twentieth birthday, she suddenly fell on her face in her bedroom, unable to move. Lupus, an autoimmune disorder, had caused a massive brain injury, and in the time it takes to turn a radio dial, she became a quadriplegic. She couldn't move her arms or her legs. Just the week before, she had purchased new running shoes.*
>
> *How do you explain such a tragedy? Is this how God honors his chosen?*
>
> *And as you're thinking of her situation, how do you explain yours? The tension at home. The demands at school. The pain of words that sting and people that laugh at your expense. Lupus may not have struck you down, but aren't you occasionally struck by God's silence? He knows what you are facing. How do we explain this?*
>
> *Maybe God messed up. Cancer cells crept into your DNA when he wasn't looking. He was so occupied with the tsunami in Asia that he forgot the famine in Uganda. He tried to change the stubborn streak in your father but just couldn't get him to budge. Honestly. A bumbling Creator? An absent-minded Maker? What evidence does Scripture provide to support such a view? What evidence does creation offer? Can't the Maker of*

heaven and earth fix bad situations and prevent natural disasters? Of course he can. Then why doesn't he?

Bible Study Discussion (15 minutes)

Say: **"Let's stop right there and add this thought to our discussion."** Then ask the following questions:

- **"Skeptics have argued that an all-powerful God could stop evil and that a loving and kind Creator would stop evil. However, their reasoning goes, since suffering and tragedies continue unabated in this often cruel world, either God isn't all-powerful or he isn't truly good, or—perhaps—he simply doesn't exist."**

- **"Comment on this argument and logic. Do you agree or not?"**

In the *It's Not About Me, Teen Edition* book, Max quotes Psalm 103 to combat the suggestion that God lets us go through hard times because he's mad at us.

> *GOD is sheer mercy and grace;*
> *not easily angered, he's rich in love.*
> *He doesn't endlessly nag and scold,*
> *nor hold grudges forever.*
> *He doesn't treat us as our sins deserve,*
> *nor pay us back in full for our wrongs.*
> *As high as heaven is over the earth,*
> *so strong is his love to those who fear him.*
> *(Psalm 103:8–11 MSG)*

- **"What does this passage suggest about the character of God?"**

Max quotes our Creator in Psalm 50: *"Trust me in your times of trouble, and I will rescue you, and you will give me glory" (Psalm 50:15 NLT).*

- **"What does this statement reveal about God, about suffering, about living for God's glory?"**

Max goes on to discuss an incident recorded in John 9: *"As [Jesus] passed by, He saw a man blind from birth. And His disciples asked Him, 'Rabbi, who sinned, this man or his parents, that he would be born blind?' Jesus answered, 'It was neither that this man sinned, nor his parents; but it was so that the works of God might be displayed in him' (John 9:1–3 NASB).*

- **"What is the 'big idea' of these verses?"**

LEADER'S NOTES:

Leader's Notes:

Remember, breaking into and out of groups takes time.

Read the first question aloud. After most of the pairs have had time to discuss it, move on to the next question, and so forth.

Max concludes with these statements:

> *God will use whatever he wants to display his glory. Heavens and stars. History and nations. People and problems.*
>
> *A season of suffering is a small assignment when compared to the reward. Rather than begrudge your problem, explore it. Ponder it. And most of all, use it. Use it to the glory of God.*

Have the group break into groups of two to three and briefly discuss these questions:

- **Do you agree that life is filled with frustration, and that nobody breezes through this world without problems and struggles? Why or why not?**
- **How do you react to the idea that God allows or orchestrates certain trials in our lives in order that we might showcase his glory?**
- **Why are some people laid back and able to flex and adapt (and perhaps even laugh) in the face of difficulties, while others just come unglued? Which kind of person are you?**

Drama/Role Play *(5 minutes)*

Get a couple (or more) of thespian-type folks (preferably a male and a female) to come forward and to improvise each of these common reactions to problems. (They should try to be funny.) Write each reaction on a slip of paper, and put all the slips in a box. Your first actor should draw a slip of paper. Then, after you read the "scenario," he or she should react according to the description on his or her paper. After thirty seconds or so, the audience should try to name the reaction.

To set the scene, say: **"Put yourself in this person's shoes—what's the reaction? You have just opened a letter in which your girlfriend/boyfriend says, 'I don't love you anymore, and I'm breaking up with you.' Then he or she adds, 'I'm in love with your best friend.'"**

Taking turns, have your actors role-play these reactions (after they draw them out of the box).

- Living in denial
- Looking for some kind of escape, diversion, amusement, or way to "medicate" my discomfort
- Whining and complaining a lot
- Getting bitter and looking for a way to lash out
- Gritting teeth and "bravely" trying to soldier on/gut it out
- Trying to figure things out rationally—"Why? Why?"
- Blaming God, other, myself, and the devil

- Thanking God in all things
- Taking the approach "What are you trying to say to me/teach me through this, God?"
- Determining in my heart to glorify God

Practical Application (5 minutes)

Hand out copies of the "Pain-O-Meter" (see the reproducible sheet on page 93). Tell everyone to rank the following situations from 1 to 4.

Pain-O-Meter

_____ Chronic (long-term) health problems
_____ Academic failure
_____ Having to relocate to a new city/school
_____ Death of a dream
_____ Dissolution of parents' marriage
_____ Death of a parent or a sibling
_____ Becoming a paraplegic/quadriplegic
_____ Being the victim of a crime
_____ Betrayal by a close friend
_____ Not being able to pursue the sport/hobby you love
_____ Being dumped by a sweetheart
_____ Feeling all alone and friendless
_____ Not making a team or not being accepted in a club you really value
_____ Financial disaster for your family (layoffs, bankruptcy, etc.)
_____ Feeling abandoned by God
_____ Contracting a debilitating disease
_____ Being falsely accused of a crime
_____ Being overweight/feeling unattractive

1. Ouch!
2. This really hurts.
3. It hurts so much I can't stop thinking about it.
4. Severe! Beyond what I can stand!

Response (15 minutes)

Hand out index cards. Tell students to take five minutes to reflect on their current life situations and to list the three biggest difficulties in their lives. After a few minutes, break into groups of four. Preselect a mature Christian student to lead each group. Encourage students to take a few risks and share their struggles, answering the following questions. Give these questions, one at a time, from the front, or print them out

LEADER'S NOTES:

Leader's Notes:

Walk among the groups, making sure that they are moving through the discussion at a good pace.

beforehand and distribute them at this time.

- **In what tough situation are you currently finding it difficult to live for God's glory?**
- **If an unbelieving friend were to ask you, "Why does God allow his people to experience such hardship and suffering?" how would you respond?**
- **How do you react when you observe someone exude genuine peace and joy in the midst of a world of trouble?**
- **Someone has suggested that apart from faith, we will never be able to reconcile God's absolute goodness, perfect wisdom, and infinite power with the suffering we face. Do you agree? Why or why not?**
- **What's more common in your life—pursuing relief from life's problems or pursuing God in the midst of problems and promoting his righteous reputation?**
- **Okay, God can get glory through our suffering. Not a fun thought. But what about us? What possible benefits can come to us from hardship? (Hint: See Romans 5:1–5 and 8:28–29.)**
- **Corrie ten Boom, a survivor from a Nazi concentration camp during World War II, once said: "When the train goes through a tunnel and the world gets dark, do you jump out? Of course not. You sit still and trust the engineer to get you through." Why is it so difficult to sit still and wait on God in tough times? In what scary or tough situations do you need to "trust the Engineer" today?**

Wrap Up

Say: **"Read along with me from *It's Not About Me, Teen Edition,* page 119."**

> *In the Intensive Care Unit, I overheard physicians warning of the worst: I might have as few as forty-eight hours to live. Dear friends and family clung to my hands, caressing limp fingers and offering disbelieving good-byes. I felt their tears fall on my arms and run down my wrists. Conscious, I marked the passage of time by the regularity of my heart monitor. I could not speak. I could not open my eyes.*
>
> This is suffering, *I declared.* This is suffering, *I said to God. I talked to him and him alone, day after excruciating day. I continually asked my only Friend,* Why?
>
> *"I consider that your present sufferings are not worth comparing with the glory that will be revealed in you," he answered.*
> *I had memorized Romans 8:18 in seventh grade Bible class, not knowing what it meant. What did I understand of glory then? What did I know of*

suffering? But I had tucked the verse away in my heart. God was packing my spiritual suitcase for a journey across the valley of the shadow of death. When those words resurfaced, I was quiet and ready to hear his whisper.

"Not worth comparing," he said as he came close.

"Not worth comparing"—the words felt like breath on the back of my neck.

"Not worth comparing," I began to say as weeks passed.

I finally was tuned in to God, and I listened. Acquaintance with suffering intensified; the characteristics of glory ever deepened in mystery. Glory is God himself. Glory revealed in us is not so much the hope of heaven or miracles wondrously unfurled in our lives but the majesty of the moment when our suffering quiets us into submission, and we realize that the Creator designs to live inside the created.

My future, my destiny, I discovered, never was a successful career but him. My purpose is God. I live, I am, and yes, I move, for him.

At one time, every dream I had treasured was irreparably broken. But amid the wreckage, I was at peace for the first time. In the center, I was still.

A decade has passed since those early hospital days, and doctors are astonished by my recovery. After months of grueling speech therapy and physical therapy, I eventually regained the ability to speak well and to walk, with a prominent limp and a cane. My dreams of delivering the nightly news are all but abandoned. It is a greater honor to deliver the good news around the world. I have shared the story of God's glory displayed in my life in Japan, Australia, Germany, Canada, and Thailand. I even taught the children of missionaries in Bangkok for almost a year.

My dearest ministry today is teaching in a public high school. I earned my degree in journalism after all, and I use it to teach English, photojournalism, and creative writing. On the first day of school, I always tell my students about the day I fell to the carpet. Mouths gape, eyes widen, and teenagers sit amazed; they cannot believe how far I have come. I pray often that my example shines with the likeness of Christ.

Mirroring God has become my career plan, my life goal. Sometimes I look at the sweet faces of my students while reminding them that life can be lost in a moment, and I am overwhelmed with blessing. A God-centered life is the highest call for living, and I would not want to be living anything less.

Nika Maples, September 2004

Hand out INAM Weekly Devotions and encourage students to complete each day.

Close the session with prayer.

Leader's Notes:

REPRODUCIBLE WORKSHEETS

for

Session 5

BUMMER BINGO

Attempt to get individuals to sign a box containing a description that truthfully describes him or her. The first person to get five signatures in a row (across, up and down, or diagonally) wins! NOTE: No one may sign a sheet more than once.

I have had a broken bone.	I have been dumped.	I have spent at least one night in a hospital.	My parents are separated or divorced.	I have had a friend or loved one die.
Someone in my family has/had cancer.	I have been fired from a job.	I have had stomach crud in the last six months.	I am allergic to some kind of food.	I have to take medication regularly.
I have been cut from a team.	I have failed a test in the last few weeks.	My best friend has moved away.	I have been robbed.	I have gotten detention at school.
I have been in a wreck.	I have had mono.	I can't see a thing without my glasses.	My house has flooded or had a fire.	One or both of my parents got laid off.
Bad Thing of your choice.	I have a disability.	I have suffered a season-ending injury.	I have been admitted to an ER in the last year.	I have moved more than three times in my life.

SCENARIOS

In groups of four, take seven minutes to answer the following questions. Begin with the person who has broken the most bones in his/her body. Proceed clockwise with each person answering one question until time runs out, or until the group or each person has answered all of the questions. Be honest!

- What would you do if . . . you were in a convenience store and a masked gunman suddenly came in to rob the place?

- What would you do if . . . someone broke a date with you to go out with one of your closest friends?

- What would you do if . . . your car broke down in the worst part of town at night—and your cell phone was dead?

- What would you do if . . . your house or apartment burned down and everything you owned was gone?

- What would you do if . . . our entire economy collapsed and we found ourselves in the middle of Great Depression II?

- What would you do if . . . you wrecked a friend's car that you weren't even supposed to be driving?

- What would you do if . . . your parent(s) announced you were moving 1,000 miles away—in 30 days?

- What would you do if . . . you discovered you had a debilitating or deadly illness (e.g. AIDS, cystic fibrosis, leukemia, ALS, cancer)?

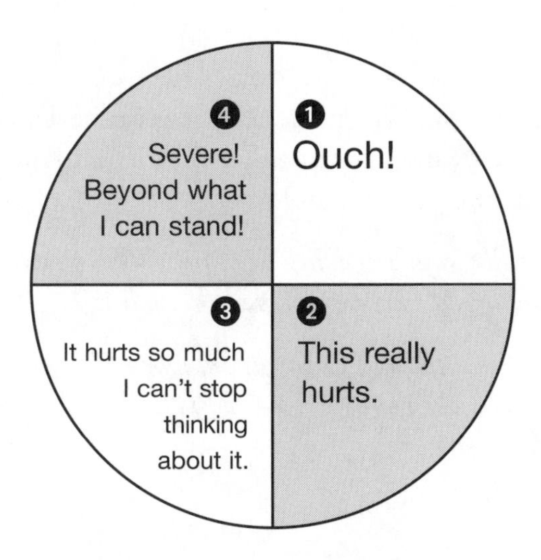

Pain-O-Meter

Rank 1 to 4, according to the Pain-O-Meter.

_____ Chronic (long-term) health problems
_____ Academic failure
_____ Having to relocate to a new city/school
_____ Death of a dream
_____ Dissolution of parents' marriage
_____ Death of a parent or a sibling
_____ Becoming a paraplegic/quadriplegic
_____ Being the victim of a crime
_____ Betrayal by a close friend
_____ Not being able to pursue the sport/hobby you love
_____ Being dumped by a sweetheart
_____ Feeling all alone and friendless
_____ Not making a team or not being accepted in a club you really value
_____ Financial disaster for your family (lay-offs, bankruptcy, etc.)
_____ Feeling abandoned by God
_____ Contracting a debilitating disease
_____ Being falsely accused of a crime
_____ Being overweight/feeling unattractive

INAM WEEKLY DEVOTIONS

Day 1

In John 11, we read the account of Lazarus. Jesus, the great healer and miracle worker, seemingly stands by and does nothing, allowing his desperately ill friend to die. Mary and Martha, the sisters of Lazarus, enter into a time of confusion and grief.

But when Jesus heard [about illness of Lazarus], He said, "This sickness is not unto death, but for the glory of God, so that the Son of God may be glorified through it."

Now Jesus loved Martha and her sister and Lazarus. So, when He heard that he was sick, He stayed two more days in the place where He was (John 11:4–6 NKJV).

What's your gut reaction to this story?

____

____

____

____

____

____

How would you feel if you were Mary or Martha, knowing that Jesus deliberately allowed your brother to die?

____

____

____

____

____

Read ahead. How does the story end? What does this suggest to you?

____

____

____

____

____

Day 2

In the midst of terrible anguish, Job cried out:

Though he slay me, yet will I hope in him (Job 13:15 NIV*).*

What is the difference between consciously *hoping* God will do something to change our suffering and subconsciously *demanding* that he do something?

Day 3

Philippians 1:29 (NIV) tells Christians, *"For it has been granted to you on behalf of Christ not only to believe on him, but also to suffer for him."*

Why should those who follow Christ not be surprised to encounter difficulties and tough times?

What is the biggest ordeal you've ever faced? The greatest tragedy?

Day 4

Take some time to meditate on the apostle Paul's experience as recorded in 2 Corinthians 4:8–18 (NLT):

We are pressed on every side by troubles, but we are not crushed and broken. We are perplexed, but we don't give up and quit. We are hunted down, but God never abandons us. We get knocked down, but we get up again and keep going. Through suffering, these bodies of ours constantly share in the death of Jesus so that the life of Jesus may also be seen in our bodies.

Yes, we live under constant danger of death because we serve Jesus, so that the life of Jesus will be obvious in our dying bodies. So we live in the face of death, but it has resulted in eternal life for you.

But we continue to preach because we have the same kind of faith the psalmist had when he said, "I believed in God, and so I speak." We know that the same God who raised our Lord Jesus will also raise us with Jesus and present us to himself along with you. All of these things are for your benefit. And as God's grace brings more and more people to Christ, there will be great thanksgiving, and God will receive more and more glory.

That is why we never give up. Though our bodies are dying, our spirits are being renewed every day. For our present troubles are quite small and won't last very long. Yet they produce for us an immeasurably great glory that will last forever! So we don't look at the troubles we can see right now; rather, we look forward to what we have not yet seen. For the troubles we see will soon be over, but the joys to come will last forever.

▶ Summarize how Paul viewed his struggles and hardships. What were the results?

____

____

____

____

____

____

▶ How does this alter the way you intend to view and respond to your struggles today?

____

____

____

____

____

____

Day 5

Don't fret or worry. Instead of worrying, pray. Let petitions and praises shape your worries into prayers, letting God know your concerns. Before you know it, a sense of God's wholeness, everything coming together for good, will come and settle you down. It's wonderful what happens when Christ displaces worry at the center of your life (Philippians 4:6–7 MSG).

The one thing you can be sure of is that . . . the God you call upon will finally come, and even if he does not bring you the answer you want, he will bring you himself. And maybe at the secret heart of all our prayers that is what we are really praying for. (Frederick Buechner)

- Are you a worrier?

- How can you roll your current burdens onto the Lord *(1 Peter 5:7)*?

Young Life® Adaptation for Session 5

Recommended for Wyldlife® Small Groups

This adaptation assumes a meeting designed primarily for enhancing relationships with students and for pre-evangelism.

After singing a couple of songs, use the opener "Bummer Bingo." Afterward, give a prize to the winner. With a smaller group (under 30 students), use "Scenarios" instead.

Next, do the *Discussion* and *Reading* sections as they are. Although they don't feature much audience involvement, they should work well.

Next, lead the group in the first part of the *Bible Study Discussio*n section, ending with the question, "What is the 'big idea' of these verses?"

Then, use the *Drama/Role Play*. It should be interesting and help illustrate common reactions to problems and difficulties.

For *Practical Application*, have everyone fill in the "Pain-O-Meter." Only ask for volunteers to share their top three and bottom three choices.

Go ahead and do *Response* as it is written, but choose just three of the questions to discuss in the groups. Choose those questions beforehand (ones that would be most appropriate for your group). Either lead the discussion as a large group, or assign an adult leader to each group, giving these leaders the questions beforehand.

Conclude with the *Wrap Up* illustration from the book (if there is time), and close in prayer.

Recommended for Young Life Campaigners

This adaptation assumes a meeting designed for Young Life Senior High Campaigner groups. The attendees will be primarily new believers with little or no church background.

Begin with the opener "Scenarios," but don't break into groups for it (7 minutes).

Next, move into *Discussion* (5 minutes).

Then do the short *Reading* (3 minutes).

Follow with *Bible Study Discussion* section (10 minutes).

Use *Practical Application* (5 minutes).

Conclude with *Response* (10 minutes).

Remind everyone of the INAM Weekly Devotions.

promoting God when life is good

Primary Lesson Texts

Deuteronomy 8:18
1 Chronicles 29:12
Proverbs 22:4
2 Corinthians 3:18

Lesson Focus/Key Concept

God gives you success so that you can make him known. (But be careful when life is good that you don't forget the source of your success!)

Lesson Goal

As a result of this meeting, students will determine to use their accomplishments and successes to point others to God.

Materials Needed

- ❑ Reproducible handouts, pages 114—120
- ❑ Pens/pencils
- ❑ Prize

LEADER'S NOTES:

Rather than one winner, you may want to give a Tootsie Pop to every person who demonstrates a unique talent.

Warmup/Openers (10 minutes)

Choose one of the following openers.

❶ Hidden Talents

Use this activity to help students gain interesting insights into each other and also to raise the subject of "gifts and abilities."

Say: **"When I say the particular 'hidden talent,' stand up if it applies to you. The first person standing must demonstrate the talent in front of everyone. That person will receive 1,000 points. Whoever has the most points at the end will get a prize."**

- Someone who knows how to safely perform the Heimlich maneuver
- Someone who can touch his or her tongue to his or her own nose
- Someone who can do the splits
- Someone who—standing and with legs straight—can touch his or her palms flat on the floor
- Someone who can turn his or her eyelids inside out
- Someone who can juggle
- Someone who can imitate Donald Duck
- Someone who can do a one-arm push-up
- Someone who can wiggle his or her ears
- Someone who can say, "I would like a salad, please" in a foreign language

❷ My Ultimate, Ideal, Perfect Week

Hand out worksheets entitled "My Ultimate, Ideal, Perfect Week!" and pens or pencils. Tell everyone to fill it in seriously. For example (use this or complete your own and show on projector):

MY ULTIMATE, IDEAL, PERFECT WEEK!

Day of the Week	Accomplishment/surprise/blessing/experience
Sunday	Experience God's touch like never before at church!
Monday	Set a personal record in the mile run!
Tuesday	Ace my algebra midterm (and even get the bonus problem right)!
Wednesday	Find out my dad got a big raise!
Thursday	Get selected by the faculty to be editor of the school paper!
Friday	Get a chance to lead a classmate to Christ!
Saturday	My band gets offered a paying gig!

Then have a brief share time, with students telling what they have written and explaining why those particular successes would make for an ideal week.

Discussion *(7 minutes)*

Introduce this by saying: "**How do you define *success*? Does it mean having certain talents and abilities? Having a lot of money? Making good grades? Being popular? Accomplishing great feats and receiving acclaim for your exploits?**

"**Does success mean having great power or influence? Achieving certain personal goals? How about enjoying a big circle of family and friends?**

"**Let's take a few minutes now to ponder our own attitudes and values when it comes to this topic of success by doing a Success Shopping Spree.**"

Distribute copies of "Success Shopping Spree" (available as a reproducible sheet) and have everyone fill out their sheets.

SUCCESS SHOPPING SPREE

Instructions: You may spend up to $100 (but not a penny more). Check the items you think would give you the greatest sense of attainment and triumph in life. Note: Shop wisely!

Items costing $25:

_____ Amazing relationship with God, marked by otherworldly peace and joy

LEADER'S NOTES:

Be prepared for some students to ask about the fairness of this exercise, questioning why they were only given certain amounts for each category.

Leader's Notes:

_____ Happy, close-knit family/home life

_____ Immensely satisfying "middle school/high school career" where I excel academically, socially, athletically

_____ Rare, highly valued ability; the chance to be among the "world's best" in a certain skill or activity (like Tiger Woods in golf or Johnny Depp in acting)

_____ Rich and wonderful dating relationship where my sweetheart and I become true soul mates

Items costing $20:

_____ Circle of lifelong, true friends—relationships marked by love and acceptance, encouragement and laughter

_____ Involvement in an amazing, dynamic, influential church—a bona fide "spiritual family"

_____ Excellent health and a long, energetic, productive life

_____ Financial prosperity—the monetary resources to do things most people only dream of

_____ Fame (being a household name, having celebrity status)

Items costing $15:

_____ Happy, lifelong marriage of my own

_____ Scholarship to prestigious "Top Five" university

_____ One day owning my own business and seeing it grow and prosper and get accolades

_____ Good looks (good complexion; a good tan; white, straight teeth)

_____ Chance to introduce many people to Christ and help them grow in their faith

Items costing $10:

_____ Completely furnished dream home in my preferred location

_____ Buff body I've always dreamed of

_____ Ability to send my children to the best schools and see them enter highly respected fields

_____ Early retirement

_____ Any car I desire

Items costing $5:

_____ After-school job that pays well and is extremely enjoyable and rewarding

_____ Ample time to pursue my hobbies and avocations (and do them well!)

_____ Opportunity to travel first-class wherever/whenever I wish

_____ Membership in certain prestigious clubs and organizations

_____ Wardrobe that is the envy of all my friends

Afterward, ask:

- **"Was this exercise more difficult than you expected? Explain."**
- **"How can an exercise like this be enlightening? Helpful?"**

Say: **"Most of us would like to 'have it all'—everything on the list. But that's not possible. And that's why we gave you only $100 to spend, to force you to make choices. Actually, in life we experience something very similar. We may try to have it all, but in reality each of us has a limited amount of resources (time, money, energy, emotions) to spend. When we say yes to certain things, we are saying no to others. How we spend our resources says a lot about what we truly value. And, if we're honest, after looking at our Success Shopping Spree sheets, we would have to admit that we don't always make the best choices."**

Reading (8 minutes)

Have two students join you in reading aloud the following short section from *It's Not About Me, Teen Edition* (see chapter 13, p. 124).

Begin by saying, **"Listen to this excerpt from *It's Not About Me, Teen Edition*."** Then read aloud section I. Instruct the students to pick up the reading where you leave off and read sections II and III.

Section I (leader)

Say: **"Max lists a few people and organizations and asks how well we know them. So let me ask, how many of you have heard of Weiden & Kennedy?"** (Ask for a show of hands after each.) **"Goodby, Silverstein and Partners?" "BBDO?" "J. Walter Thompson?"**

Explain that those are advertising agencies. They say that we may not be familiar with the companies, but we certainly are familiar with their work.

- Weiden & Kennedy created the Nike slogan, "Just Do It."
- Goodby, Silverstein and Partners created the slogan, "Got Milk?"
- "M'm! M'm! Good! M'm! M'm! Good!" was created by BBDO, the catch phrase used by Campbell's Soup since 1935.
- J. Walter Thompson wrote this jingle for Kellogg's: "Snap! Crackle! Pop!" Rice Krispies.

Leader's Notes:

These should be students who can read well and are comfortable in front of a group. Prepare them beforehand.

LEADER'S NOTES:

Then say: **"We could learn a lesson from these companies. What they do for clients, we exist to do for Christ. To live 'reflecting like mirrors the brightness of the Lord' (2 Corinthians 3:18 JB)."**

Section II (student 1)

As heaven's advertising agency, we promote God in every area of life, including success.

That's right—even your success is intended to reflect God. Listen to the reminder Moses gave the children of Israel: "Always remember that it is the LORD your God who gives you power to become rich, and he does it to fulfill the covenant he made with your ancestors" (Deuteronomy 8:18 NLT).

From where does success come? God. "It is the LORD your God who gives you power to become rich."

And why does he give it? For his reputation. "To fulfill the covenant he made with your ancestors."

God blessed Israel in order to billboard his faithfulness. When foreigners saw the fruitful farms of the Promised Land, God did not want them to think about the farmer but the farmer's Maker. Their success advertised God.

Section III (student 2)

Nothing has changed. God lets you excel so you can make him known. And you can be sure of one thing: God will make you good at something. This is his principle: "True humility and fear of the LORD lead to riches, honor, and long life" (Proverbs 22:4 NLT).

You may not be the richest kid in town, but you might be given a scholarship, an award, a good job, a pay raise. You may not be the valedictorian or drafted by the NFL, but you might be given friends or money or resources or opportunities. You will, to one degree or another, succeed. . . .

Success gives birth to amnesia. Doesn't have to, however. God offers spiritual ginseng to help your memory. His prescription is simply "Know the purpose of success." Why does God help you succeed? So you can make him known.

Bible Study Discussion (10 minutes)

Choose students who can read well.

Copy and pass out these verses and questions and ask for volunteers to read. Introduce this by saying: **"Here are the primary Bible verses that Max highlights in chapter 13 of *It's Not About Me, Teen Edition.* These nuggets of truth remind us of the true nature and purpose of *success.*"**

Then have students read the passages, one right after the other.

"And all of us . . . can be mirrors that brightly reflect the glory of the Lord. And as the Spirit of the Lord works within us, we become more and more like him and reflect his glory even more." (2 Corinthians 3:18 NLT)

"Always remember that it is the LORD your God who gives you power to become rich, and he does it to fulfill the covenant he made with your ancestors." (Deuteronomy 8:18 NLT)

"True humility and fear of the LORD lead to riches, honor, and long life." (Proverbs 22:4 NLT)

"Riches and honor come from you alone, for you rule over everything. Power and might are in your hand, and it is at your discretion that people are made great and given strength." (1 Chronicles 29:12 NLT)

Say: **"Let's wrestle with these passages for a few minutes together."** Then ask:

- **"Where does our success come from?"**
- **"Why does God give us success?"**
- **"What does 'true humility and fear of the Lord' look like in a person's everyday life?"**
- **"Someone has said, 'Humility is not looking at yourself badly; it is not looking at yourself at all.' Do you agree with this description? Why or why not?"**
- **"When have you been guilty of letting the blessings God has provided go to your head?"**

Then say: **"Max concludes:"**

> *Why does God help you succeed? So you can make him known. . . . Why are you good at what you do? For your comfort? For your wallet? For your self-esteem? No. Deem these as bonuses, not as the reason. Why are you good at what you do? For God's sake. Your success is not about what you do. It's all about him—his present and future glory.*

Drama (5 minutes)

Narrator: *Callie and her father are watching TV together—a special program about the lengths to which paparazzi will go in order to take snapshots of Hollywood's biggest stars.*

Callie: *Can you imagine living like that, Dad? Every time you go out the door, somebody's hiding in the bushes to take your picture? You just want to run to the convenience*

LEADER'S NOTES:

Be sure to have your actors rehearse this beforehand.

Leader's Notes:

store and get a drink, but suddenly you have six people with cameras and microphones following you. There are weirdos combing through your trash and writing stories in the tabloids about your likes and dislikes. Wow. I used to think I wanted to be famous—not anymore!

Callie's father: (nodding and smiling) *Yeah, fame is definitely not all it's cracked up to be. But you know, even though we don't have photographers stalking us, we do have people watching us like hawks.*

Callie: (confused) *Huh? What do you mean?*

Callie's father: *Well, think about it. You're active in the youth group. You go on a mission trip every summer. I lead a Bible study before work every Thursday morning. People watch us drive off to church every Sunday. In other words, it's no secret that we claim to be Christians. So, I guarantee you, people are watching us every day to see if we really practice what we preach, to see if our faith is real.*

Callie: *You think so?*

Callie's father: *Absolutely! The things we say, the ways we react to situations—good and bad—the way we treat people. Every day our neighbors and friends, your classmates, my co-workers are all taking mental pictures and making mental notes. And either we are a good advertisement for the claims of Christ, or not. You know, there's this one guy at work who preaches at everybody. He's always quoting the Bible and whistling Christian songs. But you know what? He's actually kind of annoying. Loud. And lots of times he's just plain rude and insensitive to others. A few months back he got promoted to a managerial position, and he became even more of a jerk.*

Callie: *Really?*

Callie's father: *Really. The bottom line is people don't like him, Callie. They talk about him behind his back. About what a hypocrite he is.*

Callie: (after a long pause) *I guess the goal then is to live in such a way that when people do watch you and talk about you, they end up saying good stuff.*

Callie's father: *Exactly. And not just good stuff about you. But good stuff about God.*

After the drama, ask:

"Consider the statements of Callie's father. Do you agree or disagree that people watch what Christians do and say? That, like it or not, we are human billboards for God?"

"Think of the Christians you know at work, school, or church. Whose life makes God look really good? Why?"

Practical Application (12 minutes)

LEADER'S NOTES:

Note: All kids have successes. Many in your group probably have experienced much "success" in school—in sports, academics, relationships, music, drama, and so forth—so they may feel comfortable with the discussion. Others, however, may feel self-conscious and even discouraged, thinking that they haven't been successful at anything or at least anything "important." So be sure to explain that everyone is successful at something.

Choose one of the following options:

❶ Success Spoof

Everyone has seen the football player who celebrates a touchdown or quarterback sack with a funky dance, or the baseball star who hits a home run and then points his index finger toward heaven as if to say, "Thanks, God! I owe it all to you."

Get three or four of your funniest, "hammiest," least self-conscious students to act out/improvise (a la *Whose Line Is It Anyway?*) how the following people might "give God glory" after successfully doing the following:

- brainy student who correctly solves a tough trig problem
- ditzy girl who just mastered a new cheerleading cheer
- plumber who successfully unclogs a toilet
- person who gets the good news of "no cavities!" from his/her dentist
- not-so-coordinated person who, after several failed efforts, manages to swallow a vitamin

❷ Commercials for God

This can be a funny and creative yet powerful, exercise. Divide into groups of four to six students (try to have at least two outgoing, creative types in each group). Tell the students they have five minutes to come up with a commercial for God (specifically for one aspect of God's character—for example, his love, power, mercy, patience). Again the point is to promote him, to get others to focus on his greatness.

Some formats students may wish to employ? Rap, skits, poems, dance, songs, mime, interview, testimonial, demonstration, "celebrity" spokesmen (good if students have certain impersonation talents).

Commercials should be thirty seconds each and have a clear message.

LEADER'S NOTES:

Illustrations (5 minutes)

Choose one of the following illustrations:

❶ Amanda

Have a student read the following abridged vignette from chapter 13 of *It's Not About Me, Teen Edition* (it begins at the bottom of page 126). Suggest that students follow along in their copies of the book.

> *Amanda Harper knows something about success—and remembers its source. Affected by congenital muscular dystrophy, Amanda missed two months of her senior year at Corona del Sol High School in Tempe, Arizona, due to chronic severe back pain—"off the charts pain," says her mother, Merlie. Finally, in January, she was able to return to school for the last semester of her senior year, armed with heavy painkillers and the "blessing" of having to take only three classes.*
>
> *Unfortunately, one of the classes was Mr. Brugger's creative writing class. . . .*
>
> *The problem was that [Mr.] Brugger insisted she write a play and submit it to the contest sponsored by VSA Arts. . . . The winning play would be performed at the John F. Kennedy Center for the Performing Arts in Washington. . . .*
>
> *Amanda freely admits she "whined and begged" to get out of the assignment. She'd never written a play before. . . . Mr. Brugger held firm. "I remember sitting next to his desk looking at the VSA brochure, and it said you could write with a partner. My ears perked up," she recounts. . . . "I went straight home and called Bethany and said, 'You have to help me graduate.'"*
>
> *Bethany Andrews is another blessing in Amanda's life. The girls first met doing volunteer work at the Christian bookstore where their mothers worked. "When we found out we both loved to write, it just clicked, and we started writing together," says Amanda. "She would spend the night at my house, and the next day our moms would go, 'What story did you make up this time?' We've written about ten stories together, not including our own stories." . . .*
>
> *Amanda's writing "trademark" is always to include at least one character with a disability, even if disability isn't the theme of the piece. Both girls share a deep curiosity about the different ways that "God made people" and were interested in portraying "hidden disability—something that isn't out there like a wheelchair." . . .*
>
> *Amanda and Bethany wrote about Haven, a high school girl who uses a wheelchair and also provides a kind of haven for other students who need a listening ear. In addition to Haven, the play features Dominic, a high school boy struggling with the hidden disability of depression. Haven wants to go to*

the prom but is convinced no one will ask her because she can't dance. The two help each other, and in the end she and Dominic go to the prom together, with him declaring, "Get ready to walk and roll!"

Amanda and Bethany's play, "Get Ready to Walk and Roll," was sent to VSA literally at the very last moment, and then promptly forgotten in the rush of graduation. In July, Amanda and Bethany were stunned to get a call saying their script had been selected from more than 170 works for a staged reading at the Kennedy Center on September 29. In addition to the onstage production, their prize included $500 each and a trip to Washington. . . .

Even though they have graduated from high school, the girls continue to write together and separately. "There are so many paths out there," Amanda muses, adding she's sure writing will be a part of whatever she does. She's thought about teaching creative writing, but at the moment her plans are simple: to "let God guide me to the place where He wants me to be."

—Christina Medvescek, October 24, 2003

Afterward ask: **"How did Amanda and Bethany demonstrate the point of this chapter?"**

❷ *Elephant Fable*

Max once related the fable of an elephant lumbering across a wooden bridge suspended over a ravine. As the big animal crossed over, the worn-out structure creaked and groaned under the elephant's immense weight. When the creature reached the other side, a flea that had nestled itself in the elephant's ear proclaimed, "Boy, did we shake that bridge!"

What's wrong with the flea's perspective? How is this an apt illustration of the way we often think and act?

Okay, true confessions time. When you "succeed" at something (whatever success happens to look like in your life), are you quick to lift your eyes heavenward and acknowledge your blessing as coming from God? Do you thank him? Or do you gloat and strut about? Do you forget him? Do you tend to see your achievements as the work of your hands? As your own doing? The result of your own intelligence and hard work?

Response *(10 minutes)*

Say: **"Success is a relative term. You may not have as much influence, wealth, or intelligence as some people, but you do have more than other people. At issue isn't the nature of our success or how much we perceive that we have or don't have. No, the real issue is what will we do with the good things God has done in us and for us."**

Then ask:

"Okay, this is no time for false modesty—what are your talents? What awards have

Leader's Notes:

Again, it takes time to break into groups, so be sure to plan for it.

LEADER'S NOTES:

you received? What blessings (relational, occupational, financial, physical) do you enjoy? What have been your greatest successes in life? Why?"

"How can you use your God-given talents to showcase God?"

"How can you use your accomplishments to talk about God in a way that doesn't sound fake or pious?"

Then choose one of the following ways to close:

❶ *Counting Our Blessings*

Divide into groups of four. Then say: **"There's an old hymn that urges, 'count your blessings . . . name them one by one.' Let's take a few minutes to do that. Specifically, focus now on your God-given abilities, talents, strengths, successes.**

"Maybe you got all A's on your last report card. Perhaps you scored the game-winning points in a recent athletic contest. Maybe you recently encouraged a discouraged friend or participated in a really powerful ministry event. The point isn't to brag on yourself but to acknowledge a specific instance in which God gave you the ability and opportunity to do something."

❷ *The Thankfulness Exercise*

Say: **"We have been created by God and for his purposes. Our job description is to honor him 24/7. This, of course, includes both bad times and good. No matter what situations we face, our mission is the same: to focus on God and to bring him glory. One way we can do this is to develop a thankful heart. People who develop an attitude of gratitude typically are . . .**

- **more optimistic, hopeful, and joyful;**
- **more likely to maintain an inner sense of peace;**
- **less 'blown away' by the trials of life; and**
- **more pleasant to be around."**

Then hand out copies of the "Thankfulness Exercise" sheet (see reproducible sheets).

Wrap Up

Close the session by gathering students in a circle and each student taking turns completing this short, "finish the sentence" prayer:

> *"God, I thank you for _____."*

Note: Not only does this exercise get students in the habit of being grateful, it also teaches them how to pray, getting them comfortable addressing God in front of others.

Hand out INAM Weekly Devotions and encourage students to complete each day.

REPRODUCIBLE WORKSHEETS

for

Session 6

MY ULTIMATE, IDEAL, PERFECT WEEK!

Day of the Week	*Accomplishment/surprise/blessing/experience*
Sunday	
Monday	
Tuesday	
Wednesday	
Thursday	
Friday	
Saturday	

SUCCESS SHOPPING SPREE

Instructions: You may spend up to $100 (but not a penny more). Check the items you think would give you the greatest sense of attainment and triumph in life. Note: Shop wisely!

Items costing $25:

______ Amazing relationship with God, marked by otherworldly peace and joy
______ Happy, close-knit family/home life
______ Immensely satisfying "middle school/high school career" where I excel academically, socially, athletically
______ Rare, highly-valued ability; the chance to be among the "world's best" in a certain skill or activity (like Tiger Woods in golf or Johnny Depp in acting)
______ Rich and wonderful dating relationship where my sweetheart and I become true soul mates

Items costing $20:

______ Circle of lifelong, true friends—relationships marked by love and acceptance, encouragement and laughter
______ Involvement in an amazing, dynamic, influential church—a bona fide "spiritual family"
______ Excellent health and a long, energetic, productive life
______ Financial prosperity—the monetary resources to do things most people only dream of
______ Fame (being a household name, having celebrity status)

Items costing $15:

______ Happy, lifelong marriage of my own
______ Scholarship to prestigious "Top Five" university
______ One day owning my own business and seeing it grow and prosper and get accolades
______ Good looks (good complexion; a good tan; white, straight teeth)
______ Chance to introduce many people to Christ and help them grow in their faith

Items costing $10:

______ Completely furnished dream home in my preferred location
______ Buff body I've always dreamed of
______ Ability to send my children to the best schools and see them enter highly respected fields
______ Early retirement
______ Any car I desire

Items costing $5:

______ After-school job that pays well and is extremely enjoyable and rewarding
______ Ample time to pursue my hobbies and avocations (and do them well!)
______ Opportunity to travel first-class wherever/whenever I wish
______ Membership in certain prestigious clubs and organizations
______ Wardrobe that is the envy of all my friends

Drama

Narrator: *Callie and her father are watching TV together—a special program about the lengths to which paparazzi will go in order to take snapshots of Hollywood's biggest stars.*

Callie: *Can you imagine living like that, Dad? Every time you go out the door, somebody's hiding in the bushes to take your picture? You just want to run to the convenience store and get a drink, but suddenly you have six people with cameras and microphones following you. There are weirdos combing through your trash and writing stories in the tabloids about your likes and dislikes. Wow. I used to think I wanted to be famous—not anymore!*

Callie's father: (nodding and smiling) *Yeah, fame is definitely not all it's cracked up to be. But you know, even though we don't have photographers stalking us, we do have people watching us like hawks.*

Callie: (confused) *Huh? What do you mean?*

Callie's father: *Well, think about it. You're active in the youth group. You go on a mission trip every summer. I lead a Bible study before work every Thursday morning. People watch us drive off to church every Sunday. In other words, it's no secret that we claim to be Christians. So, I guarantee you, people are watching us every day to see if we really practice what we preach, to see if our faith is real.*

Callie: *You think so?*

Callie's father: *Absolutely! The things we say, the ways we react to situations—good and bad—the way we treat people. Every day our neighbors and friends, your classmates, my co-workers are all taking mental pictures and making mental notes. And either we are a good advertisement for the claims of Christ, or not. You know, there's this one guy at work who preaches at everybody. He's always quoting the Bible and whistling Christian songs. But you know what? He's actually kind of annoying. Loud. And lots of times he's just plain rude and insensitive to others. A few months back he got promoted to a managerial position, and he became even more of a jerk.*

Callie: *Really?*

Callie's father: *Really. The bottom line is people don't like him, Callie. They talk about him behind his back. About what a hypocrite he is.*

Callie: (after a long pause) *I guess the goal then is to live in such a way that when people do watch you and talk about you, they end up saying good stuff.*

Callie's father: *Exactly. And not just good stuff about you. But good stuff about God.*

THANKFULNESS EXERCISE

Use this handout to remind you of the countless ways God has been good to you. Don't feel confined to this list. Be creative and express whatever is on your heart. "God, I thank you for . . ."

Spiritual blessings:

"for forgiving my sins"
"for adopting me into your family"
"for taking my guilt and shame"
"for giving me your Word"
"for the promise of heaven"
"for choosing me"
"for loving me"
"for sending Christ to die in my place"
"for giving me a new nature"
"for giving me your Holy Spirit"
"for giving me a loving youth group/church"
"for power to overcome temptation"

Relational blessings:

"for __________ (name a family member or beloved relative)"

"for __________ (my parents)"

"for __________ (name a friend or two)"

"for __________ (my youth leader)"

"for __________ (list a teacher or two)"

Emotional blessings:

"for smiles"
"for encouraging words"
"for faithful friends"
"for hugs"
"for beauty"

Cultural blessings:

"for freedom"
"for art"
"for our national, civic heritage"
"for music"

Material/financial blessings:

"for the basic necessities of life (food, clothing, shelter)"
"for other luxuries and comforts (vehicles, air conditioning, phones, hot showers)"
"for money to live and to give"
"for college funds/tuition, scholarships, grants"
"for E-mail, cell phones"

Personal blessings:

"for my God-given abilities and strengths"
"for my appearance"
"for my mind"
"for my unique personality"
"for my sense of humor"
"for my pets"

INAM WEEKLY DEVOTIONS

Day 1

What this means is that those who become Christians become new persons. They are not the same anymore, for the old life is gone. A new life has begun! (2 Corinthians 5:17 NLT).

But to all who believed him and accepted him, he gave the right to become children of God (John 1:12 NLT).

The Bible asserts that when we believe in Christ, we are radically changed within. We become new people, and we gain a new, true identity as children of God. In other words, in a spiritual but very real sense, when you put your faith in Jesus, you become a forever member of the ultimate "royal family."

How much of your heavenly Father's character does the world see in you? Are you helping or hindering God's reputation? How do you know?

Day 2

But the fruit of the Spirit is love, joy, peace, patience, kindness, goodness, faithfulness, gentleness and self-control (Galatians 5:22-23 NIV).

Using the "fruit of the Spirit" (above) as a kind of measuring stick, how well are you reflecting God's glorious nature to a watching world? Circle the number that best fits how you most often reflect each "spiritual fruit."

	Poor				Average			Excellent		
Love	1	2	3	4	5	6	7	8	9	10
Joy	1	2	3	4	5	6	7	8	9	10
Peace	1	2	3	4	5	6	7	8	9	10
Patience	1	2	3	4	5	6	7	8	9	10
Kindness	1	2	3	4	5	6	7	8	9	10
Goodness	1	2	3	4	5	6	7	8	9	10
Faithfulness	1	2	3	4	5	6	7	8	9	10
Gentleness	1	2	3	4	5	6	7	8	9	10
Self-control	1	2	3	4	5	6	7	8	9	10

- What specifically can you do to bring up your scores in these areas?

Day 3

Writing to some Christians in ancient Corinth, the apostle Paul said: *"We are therefore Christ's ambassadors, as though God were making his appeal through us" (2 Corinthians 5:20 NIV).*

- What exactly does an ambassador do? Why is he or she important? How can a bad ambassador really make a mess of things?

- What's the job description for an "ambassador for Christ"? What's the most challenging part of being a representative of God?

Day 4

Pride goes before destruction, and haughtiness before a fall (Proverbs 16:18 NLT).

- What is pride? How would you define it to a child?

- Why do we get prideful when God blesses us?

Day 5

They did not conquer the land with their swords; it was not their own strength that gave them victory. It was by your mighty power that they succeeded; it was because you favored them and smiled on them (Psalm 44:3 NLT).

For who makes you different from anyone else? What do you have that you did not receive? And if you did receive it, why do you boast as though you did not? (1 Corinthians 4:7 NIV).

- How do these verses (or how *should* these verses) eliminate the attitude of pride from our lives?

In the space below, list all of the good gifts God has dropped into your life—all the blessings, all the ways he has shown you favor. Then go through your list, item by item, thanking God for each entry and asking him to help you use that experience or expertise or possession or relationship for his glory.

Young Life® Adaptation for Session 6

Recommended for Wyldlife® Small Groups

This adaptation assumes a meeting designed primarily for enhancing relationships with students and for pre-evangelism.

Open with "Hidden Talents" and give a prize to the winner.

Next, do the *Discussion* as presented. Be prepared, however, for complaints and comments as students fill out the "Success Shopping Spree" sheets. Many will not like the idea of having to make the choices, especially those high achievers who want to be successful in all areas of their lives. As your first discussion question, you may want to ask: "How would your choices change if you had another $100 to spend?" and "Why do you think we limited the amount to $100?"

Many students in your group may have experienced some "success" in school—in sports, academics, relationships, music, drama, and so forth—so they may feel comfortable with the discussion. Others, however, may feel self-conscious and even discouraged, thinking that they haven't been successful at anything, or at least anything "important." Explain that everyone is successful at something.

Use the *Reading* section as it is.

Next, have students (chosen and prepared ahead of time) stand and read aloud the Bible verses in the *Bible Study Discussion* section.

Then move to the *Drama* section and have two students act out the scene. Discuss the presentation using the questions provided.

For *Practical Application*, either option should work well. "Success Spoof" is lighter than "Commercials for God," so choose the one that best fits your group.

Next, read and discuss the "Elephant Fable" illustration (rather than "Amanda," which students may find a bit long and heavy.) You ought to be able to get good discussion following the "Elephant Fable."

For *Response*, either option should work well. The first one, "Counting Our Blessings," is probably the most nonthreatening and less time-consuming.

Close in prayer.

Recommended for Young Life Campaigners

This adaptation assumes a meeting designed for Young Life Senior High Campaigner groups. The attendees will be primarily new believers with little or no church background.

Do the *Discussion* on your definition of success (10–12 minutes).

Use the *Reading* section as it is (8 minutes).

Next, in the *Bible Study Discussion*, read the verses and discuss the questions at the end of this section (20–30 minutes).

Ask only one or two of the questions in *Response* (10–12 minutes). Then talk about being thankful in all circumstances and conclude with the students taking turns completing this short "finish the sentence" prayer: "God, I thank you for ____________________."

Remind everyone of the INAM Weekly Devotions.